Featuring whimsical, delicious and enchanting desserts, *Sweet Bake Shop* has the perfect recipes for every moment whether it be a weekday craving or a special occasion. Discover how to bake irresistible and easy-to-make layer cakes and cupcakes including a pink sprinkle-covered Vanilla Birthday Cake and Raspberry Ripple Cupcakes topped with buttery vanilla frosting. Impress your friends with a fresh batch of cookies, perhaps Tessa's favourite Vanilla Bean Shortbread or Giant Gingerbread Cuties, and expand your sugar cookie skills to make magical sweets like Pretty Pastel Pony Cookies and Polka Dot Bunny Cookies. There are so many delightful treats to whip up, from adorable Cotton Candy Cloud Macarons and Fuzzy Peach Macarons to decadent Cookie Dough Scoops and Overnight Oreo Party Popcorn. *Sweet Bake Shop* also offers easy-to-follow tutorials, expert tips, baking techniques and a list of the essential tools and ingredients for your baking success. Tessa's helpful guidance and delectable desserts will inspire the baker in all of us.

Sweet Bake Shop

Delightful Desserts for the Sweetest of Occasions

Tessa Sam

PENGUIN

an imprint of Penguin Canada, a division of Penguin Random House Canada Limited

Canada • USA • UK • Ireland • Australia • New Zealand • India • South Africa • China

First published 2018

www.penguinrandomhouse.ca

LIBRARY AND ARCHIVES CANADA CATALOGUING IN PUBLICATION

Sam, Tessa, author
    Sweet bake shop : delightful desserts for the sweetest of occasions / Tessa Sam.

Issued in print and electronic formats.
ISBN 978-0-7352-3291-4 (hardcover).—ISBN 978-0-7352-3292-1 (electronic)

1. Desserts. 2. Baking. 3. Cookbooks. I. Title.

TX773.S25 2018   641.86   C2017-902433-7
C2017-902434-5

Food photography by Tessa Sam
Part openers and lifestyle photography by Blush Wedding Photography

Cover and interior design by Jennifer Lum
Front cover image by Tessa Sam
Back cover image by Blush Wedding Photography

Printed and bound in China

10 9 8 7 6 5 4 3 2 1

Penguin
Random House
PENGUIN CANADA

For my parents,

who will most likely bake these recipes with healthy modifications

and then call me to say that their cakes taste funny.

Contents

Cupcake Cravings

Gourmet Cookies

Sugar Cookies Galore

Decorating Sugar Cookies with Royal Icing 110

Whimsical Treats

Marvellous Macarons

⌒ ♡ ⌒

Frostings and Fillings

Introduction

remember it like it was yesterday. I was sitting at my desk, staring blankly at my computer screen, trying to muster some sort of excitement about my job. Here I was, having landed a "dream job" right out of broadcasting school, and I was miserable. How did I get here? Hadn't I wanted this?

My whole life up until that point, I'd loved to do two things: talk and bake. The talking came first. One of my earliest childhood memories is of climbing onto the bathroom counter and playing "TV announcer," talking to my reflection in the mirror and using a hairbrush as a microphone.

Around age two, I began helping my parents in the kitchen. It didn't matter what we were baking, I was just happy to take part in the sugary process. I would stand on my stepstool at the kitchen counter and wait to lick the spoon, then plop myself on the floor in front of the oven and watch the dessert bake.

By age ten, I'd roped my best friend into baking with me, and on weekends during the summers following, we would sell our creations at a little stand my dad made for us, at the end of my driveway. Those easy days spent eating more raw cookie dough than anyone should are some of my fondest memories. But of course, all good things must come to an end. I became a teenager, and baking wasn't cool anymore (um, not that I was ever cool), so I turned off the oven for good—or so I thought.

In high school, I was frequently scolded for talking in all my classes, often finding myself in detention writing lines. So naturally, when it came time to decide what to choose in the way of post-secondary education, it seemed a natural choice to get paid to talk.

I graduated from broadcasting school and landed a job as an on-air co-host at a radio station. It was exciting at first, but the shiny newness of my job quickly wore off and I found myself deeply unhappy. It is terrifying to realize that you are somewhere you shouldn't be, especially after working so hard to get there. I kept pushing through it, though, ignoring the little voice inside my head that was telling me I didn't belong. That was, until one morning, I did listen—and left the radio world behind.

I went back to my job as a waitress and picked up some part-time work at a bakery. It was there, surrounded by bowls of buttercream, covered in flour and working long, unglamorous hours, that something clicked: this was my happy place.

I eventually gave up both jobs and started my own company, Sweet Bake Shop, run out of my apartment kitchen in downtown Vancouver. I set up a website and took orders via email, and customers would pick up their sweets at my front door.

A few years later, I attended the Peggy Porschen Academy in London, England—a dream of mine for years—to really hone my skills in cookie decorating and specialty cake design. By 2014, I was having a difficult time keeping up with orders and knew that I needed to take my home-based business to the next level.

But of course, my modest bank account was no match for the expense of opening a bakery. Then one evening, my boyfriend at the time came home with a cheque in hand. In an act of incredible generosity, he'd sold his beloved company watch and was giving me the money to start my business. (He remains a great friend.)

I leased a small space, purchased some old pieces of furniture and began months of sanding, filling, priming and painting, everything from the walls to the front counters, until everything looked perfect. I roped my boyfriend into helping, promising to pay him in cupcakes for the rest of his life (because that's really all I could afford). To save money, I went to restaurant-equipment auctions in cold, creepy warehouses in the suburbs, and bought the pieces I would need. As the bakery began to come together, I wrote up a menu and hired staff.

That summer, I opened Sweet Bake Shop, a boutique bakery just a few blocks from my apartment, and I couldn't have been more excited. The first few months were a blur of cake crumbs and little sleep. On more than one occasion, I found myself spending the night in my shop, napping on a piece of flattened cardboard, so that I could keep an eye on cake layers baking in the oven. Oh, the glamorous life of a new business owner!

Bakery life was a lot of fun, but eventually other opportunities came knocking, and I made the decision to close the doors to my storefront shop to pursue them. These days, things are a little less hectic. I teach baking workshops, film videos for my YouTube channel and keep up with my blog and social media. I also still enjoy spending time in the kitchen, whipping up sweets for weddings and parties.

It's often said that when you know something (or someone) is right for you, you just know—and I knew, that first summer I spent working in a bakery ten years ago. This sugary world that brings so much joy to so many is where I'm meant to be, and I'm so happy that I'm able to share it with you. To me, there is something so magical about being in the kitchen, creating something beautiful and delicious. Baking is my happy place, my escape from the day-to-day, and the thing that never disappoints (unless it's a failed batch of macarons!).

In this book, I aim to provide a fun approach to baking, beginning with my list of accessible, top-quality ingredients. Some of the recipes you'll find here are fairly straightforward, while others are more challenging. Whatever your skill level, know that everyone starts somewhere, and practice is the key to improvement.

My whole heart (and a whole lot of sugar, butter and flour) went into the making of this book. Here, you'll find recipes that remind me of my childhood, plus those for the best-selling sweets from my shop and, of course, a few new desserts that I absolutely love—and I hope you'll love them, too.

Happy baking!

♡ Tessa

Baking Tools, Techniques and Ingredients

Bake Shop Tools

These are the tools you'll find in my kitchen at all times—and ones I can't live (or at least bake) without.

Offset Metal Spatulas	Offset spatulas can be found in a variety of sizes. They're perfect for applying frosting to both the inside and the outside of cakes, as well as for moving cakes from a turntable to a box or serving plate.
Cake Scrapers	A cake scraper is the ultimate tool for creating smooth sides and crisp edges on cake frostings. When used with a turntable, the results can yield icing perfection.
Rubber Spatulas	Rubber spatulas are one of the most used tools in my kitchen. There truly is nothing better for folding batter, scraping down bowls or mixing in flavourings and food colours.
Piping Tips	From icing cookies to piping macarons to frosting cupcakes, piping tips get the job done right. They come in a wide variety of shapes and sizes, with the smaller ones typically used for piping small details on cookies and the larger for topping cupcakes with glorious swirls.
Pastry Bags	Disposable or reusable, the choice is yours. Most often, I use the disposable plastic variety, especially when working with royal icing, as any greasy residue from a frosting can keep royal icing from drying properly.
Wooden Spoons	Wooden spoons are wonderful for the jobs done over the stove. Because they are heatproof, they have no problem tackling hot recipes, such as compote and caramel.
Silicone Macaron Mats	Silicone mats with circular templates allow for uniform piping, resulting in macarons of the same size and shape. If you don't have a mat with circular templates, you can trace the templates provided (page 206) onto a piece of parchment paper and slip it underneath your mat before piping the macaron batter.
Cake Boards	Cake boards provide a sturdy base for cakes, allowing them to be lifted and transported easily. They're available in a variety of sizes and finishes and can be found in most craft and baking supply stores.
Kitchen Scales	For the most accurate measurements, a kitchen scale is key. Weighing ingredients, especially dry ingredients such as flour and sugar, eliminates the chance of over- or under-measuring, ensuring consistent baking results.
Serrated Knife	I keep a long serrated knife on hand at all times. It's perfect for levelling and splitting cake layers, as well as chopping up chocolate chips.

Spring-Loaded Ice Cream Scoops	These handy scoops aren't just for ice cream. They're perfect for scooping precise amounts of cookie dough and cupcake batter too, resulting in almost identical-sized treats.
Sifter	A fantastic tool for aerating dry ingredients and eliminating any clumps. I always sift cake flour and almond flour, though I don't always find it necessary to sift other flours or confectioners' sugar.
Pastry Brush	A pastry brush is a great tool for greasing cake pans with butter. Whether you use one with natural bristles or ones made of silicone is up to you.
Cake Turntable	This handy tool can be found in the kitchen of almost every cake decorator. A cake is set in the centre of the platform and is rotated gently while a cake scraper gets to work smoothing and straightening the frosting on the outside.
Stand Mixer	The ultimate mixing machine. Most recipes in this book call for the use of a stand mixer. If you'll be using a hand mixer instead, know that mixing times may be longer and could alter the outcome of your desserts.

Bake It Better

These are four of the most important baking tips that will help you turn out perfect bakes every time.

Sift It Don't skip sifting if the recipe calls for it. This process helps to aerate dry ingredients, which creates fluffier desserts. Additionally, it eliminates any clumps.

Have Ingredients at Room Temperature Ignoring the "room temperature" instruction can result in a less than lovely product. Simply put, warm ingredients just blend better. Allowing your butter, eggs and milk to come to room temperature before using them helps them mix together seamlessly, creating a smooth batter (or dough or frosting) and a perfect dessert.

Weigh Dry Ingredients One of the best things I ever did was purchase a digital kitchen scale. For years, I used the "scoop and level" method of measuring: I would scoop the measuring cup into the dry ingredients and then level it off with the side of a knife. The problem with this method is that it's not accurate or consistent, and sometimes I would end up with cakes and cookies that were dry. Weighing my ingredients eliminated this problem completely, and now whenever I bake, I always use my scale.

Grease Your Cake Pans Dealing with a cake layer that won't budge out of its pan is so frustrating! Be sure to take the time to brush your cake pans with butter, coat them in flour and apply a parchment circle to the bottom, before you pour in the batter—and your cake layers will come out with ease. See page 12 for a visual tutorial on how to properly grease cake pans.

Essential Ingredients

These are what I consider the key ingredients that you'll want to have on hand for baking.

Dutch-Processed Cocoa Powder	This dark, delicious cocoa powder creates deeply flavourful baked goods. In a pinch, you can substitute natural cocoa powder for the recipes in this book, but for best results, pick up some of the Dutch version.
Vanilla	I'm a big fan of vanilla and use it as often as I can. I use both pure vanilla extract and vanilla bean paste in my recipes, and my brand of choice is Nielsen-Massey.
Food Colouring	I prefer gel food colouring over liquid, mostly because it doesn't water down the consistency of what I'm adding it to. Plus, it tends to have a super-concentrated colour, which allows me to use less and replace the bottle less often. My favourite brand of gel food colouring is AmeriColor.

Chocolate Chips	Some people like to keep a block of chocolate in their cupboard for baking, but I prefer chocolate chips because they're so much more convenient. I find that semi-sweet chips work well in almost every recipe. Bernard Callebaut is my absolute favourite brand.
Butter	Always use unsalted butter unless the recipe calls for salted. (Salty frosting is less than appetizing!) Also, for optimum texture, be sure to give your butter a few hours to soften or come to room temperature before using it in a recipe.
Flour	All-purpose flour and cake flour are the most commonly used flours in this book, followed by almond flour and bread flour. These flours are *not* interchangeable, so be sure to have the correct ones on hand before beginning a recipe.
Baking Soda and Baking Powder	Don't substitute one for the other, and replace them every few months as they tend to lose their leavening power over time.
Salt	Kosher salt is always best, as it is free of iodine and anti-caking agents, but table salt or sea salt will do in a pinch. Be sure to store it away from heat and moisture to prevent pesky clumps from forming.
Sugar	Brown, granulated and confectioners' are three sugars that I always have in my pantry. They all serve different purposes and are *not* interchangeable, so be sure to stock up on the ones you'll need before beginning a recipe.
Eggs	The eggs in this book are always large size and always used at room temperature. To bring eggs to room temperature quickly, place them in a bowl of hot (but not boiling) water for about 5 minutes.
Milk	Milk and buttermilk are the two most used milks in this book. For the best results, be sure to purchase the full-fat version of each. For optimum results, always bring milk to room temperature before using it in a recipe.
Meringue Powder	I use this magic powder in my Royal Icing (page 194) in place of egg whites. Using raw egg (pasteurized or not) in an uncooked recipe makes me nervous (potential salmonella), and this powder is the perfect thing to set the icing to firm perfection.
Sprinkles	Jimmies, nonpareils, confetti sequins, dragées … whatever your choice, sprinkles always add a little pop of colour and fun to desserts.

Lovely Layer Cakes

Baking a Better Cake

Greasing a Cake Pan

1. Begin by using a pastry brush to lightly coat the inside of a cake pan with softened or melted butter.

2. Add a few tablespoons of flour and tap it around the inside of the pan until all the buttered surface is covered, then turn the pan upside down over a sink or garbage can and tap out the excess flour.

3. Cut out a circle of parchment paper and place it on the bottom of the pan, to prevent the bottom of the cake from sticking.

How to Level, Split, Fill and Frost a Cake

Whipping up a cake with even layers and perfectly smooth sides isn't as difficult as you may think. All it takes are the right tools and a little practice.

1. Begin by placing a cake layer on a turntable. Gently rest your hand on top of the cake and, using a long serrated knife, score the cake along the top of the side, where the dome starts.

2. Slowly spin the turntable and begin cutting into and across the cake, keeping the knife as level as possible. Once you reach the centre of the cake, the dome will be completely detached and should lift away with ease.

3. If your recipe calls for the cake to be split into two layers, score the levelled cake halfway up the side and begin cutting into it while spinning the turntable.

4. Remove the cake from the turntable. Place a nonslip square in the middle of the turntable and then centre a cake board on top. Apply a small dollop of frosting to the middle of the cake board (this will secure the cake in place) and place a cake layer, cut side up, on top. Use an offset spatula to evenly spread your frosting, about ½ inch thick, smoothing as best you can. Place another cake layer on top and repeat.

5. Place the final cake layer on the stack upside down, so that the bottom is facing up, providing a flat top for your cake. Press down lightly to help it stick to the frosting.

6. Apply a thin layer of frosting all the way around the cake, from top to bottom, scraping off the excess with a cake scraper. This is called a crumb coat, and it catches any crumbs so that they don't end up in your final layer of frosting. Place in the refrigerator until chilled and set, about 30 minutes.

7. Apply a thicker layer of frosting all the way around the cake, from top to bottom.

8. Use a cake scraper to smooth the frosting, making sure to keep the scraper parallel to the side of the cake, with the bottom resting directly on the turntable, spinning it as you go.

9. Remove and smooth the extra frosting at the top of the cake with an offset spatula. Pull the frosting from the outside lip of the cake inwards, towards your body, in one smooth, level motion, working your way around the cake until it is smooth and flat.

10. Decorate and enjoy.

Preparing a Pastry Bag

1. Begin by snipping the tip off of a large pastry bag. Insert a piping tip and push it down to fit against the hole you've just cut. The whole end of the piping tip should be exposed.

2. Fold the edges of the bag over your hand, or place it inside a tall glass and fold the edges over the rim. Use a rubber spatula to half fill the bag (over-filling can cause frosting to spill out of the bag).

3. Fold up the edges of the bag, twist the top to close it, and you are all set to pipe.

Dreamy Vanilla Cake

Fluffy, moist and packed with vanilla goodness, this cake is what my dessert dreams are made of. It pairs well with almost any frosting or filling, but my favourites are the Bake Shop Vanilla Frosting (page 190) as shown here and the Cake Batter Frosting (page 193).

Makes three 8-inch round cake layers

4¼ cups (485 g) cake flour, sifted, plus more for pans

2¼ cups (450 g) granulated sugar

5 teaspoons baking powder

½ teaspoon salt

1 cup (225 g) unsalted butter, cut into pieces, room temperature, plus more for pans

1½ cups buttermilk, room temperature

2½ teaspoons pure vanilla extract

5 large egg whites, room temperature

1 large egg, room temperature

Cake Variations

Vanilla Birthday Cake (page 28)

Lemon Blueberry Cake (page 48)

Cupcake Variations

French Cupcakes (page 60)

Sprinkly Vanilla Party Cupcakes (page 59)

1. Preheat the oven to 350°F (180°C). Grease and flour three 8-inch round cake pans and line with parchment circles.

2. In the bowl of a stand mixer fitted with the paddle attachment, combine the flour, sugar, baking powder and salt. Mix on low speed until blended. With the mixer running on low speed, add the butter, a few pieces at a time, mixing until the mixture is crumbly.

3. In a small bowl, whisk together the buttermilk and vanilla. With the mixer running on low speed, pour two-thirds of the buttermilk mixture into the bowl and mix until the batter comes together. Turn the mixer up to medium speed and beat for about 90 seconds, until the batter has gained volume. Stop the mixer and scrape down the sides and bottom of the bowl with a rubber spatula.

4. Add the egg whites and egg to the remaining buttermilk mixture and whisk together with a fork. Pour half of the egg mixture into the bowl and mix on low speed until some of the liquid has been incorporated, then beat on medium speed to combine completely, 15 to 20 seconds. Stop the mixer, add the remaining egg mixture and beat for an additional 15 seconds on medium speed.

5. Divide the batter evenly among the prepared pans, smoothing with the back of a spoon until even and bake for 23 to 25 minutes, until a toothpick inserted in the centre of the cakes comes out clean. Allow the cakes to cool in their pans for about 20 minutes before turning them out onto a wire rack. Remove the parchment paper from the bottom of each cake, turn them right side up and leave them to cool completely.

6. Cake layers will keep at cool room temperature, wrapped tightly in plastic wrap, for up to 24 hours.

Ultimate Chocolate Cake

When I first began taking orders from home and buying baking ingredients, a happy accident occurred—the wrong type of cocoa powder was delivered. I had ordered a natural cocoa powder, which is light in colour and fairly acidic, but instead ended up with Dutch-processed cocoa powder, which is darker and has a neutral acidity. I altered my recipe slightly to best suit the new cocoa powder, and the result was so delicious, I never looked back. Shown here paired with Bake Shop Vanilla Frosting (page 190), this cake is so versatile and pairs well with almost any frosting or filling. Try it with the Eggless Chocolate Chip Cookie Dough (page 197), Bake Shop Vanilla Frosting, caramel variation (page 190) or simply with my Vanilla Bean Whipped Cream (page 199).

Makes three 8-inch round cake layers

Unsalted butter, for greasing pans

2½ cups (315 g) all-purpose flour, plus more for pans

2 cups (400 g) granulated sugar

1½ cups (165 g) Dutch-processed cocoa powder

2 teaspoons baking soda

1 teaspoon baking powder

½ teaspoon salt

⅓ cup (60 g) semi-sweet chocolate chips

2 cups whole milk, room temperature

½ cup sour cream

½ cup vegetable oil

2 large eggs, room temperature

1 teaspoon pure vanilla extract

Cake Variations

Cookie Dough Chocolate Sprinkle Cake (page 34)

Summer Party Cake (page 40)

Chocolate Sprinkle Cake (page 31)

Cupcake Variation

Carnival Caramel Popcorn Cupcakes (page 71)

1. Preheat the oven to 350°F (180°C). Grease and flour three 8-inch round cake pans and line with parchment circles.

2. In the bowl of a stand mixer fitted with the paddle attachment, combine the flour, sugar, cocoa powder, baking soda, baking powder and salt. Mix on low speed until blended.

3. In a heatproof bowl set over a saucepan of simmering water, melt the chocolate chips, stirring often with a rubber spatula to prevent burning. Remove the bowl from the pan and set aside.

4. In a medium bowl, whisk together the milk, sour cream, vegetable oil, eggs and vanilla. Pour the mixture into the bowl with the dry ingredients, then add the melted chocolate. Mix on low speed until the mixture comes together, then turn up to medium speed and beat for about 30 seconds. Stop the mixer and scrape down the sides and bottom of the bowl with a rubber spatula, then beat again on medium speed for an additional 10 seconds.

5. Divide the batter evenly among the prepared cake pans and bake for 25 to 30 minutes, until a toothpick inserted in the centre of the cakes comes out clean. Allow the cakes to cool in their pans for 20 minutes before turning them out onto a wire rack. Remove the parchment paper from the bottom of each cake, turn them right side up and leave them to cool completely.

6. Cake layers will keep at cool room temperature, wrapped tightly in plastic wrap, for up to 24 hours.

Best Banana Cake

This super-moist cake is a cross between banana bread and cake! Shown here with Cream Cheese Frosting (page 191), it's equally tasty with Bake Shop Vanilla Frosting (page 190) or a simple drizzle of Chocolate Ganache (page 196).

Makes three 8-inch round cake layers

3 cups (345 g) cake flour, sifted, plus more for pans

2 cups (400 g) granulated sugar

2 teaspoons cinnamon

2 teaspoons baking soda

1 teaspoon baking powder

1 teaspoon salt

1½ cups mashed ripe banana (about 4 medium bananas)

1 cup whole milk, room temperature

½ cup sour cream

¼ cup vegetable oil

¼ cup (55 g) unsalted butter, melted, plus more for pans

¼ cup hot water

2 large eggs, room temperature

2 teaspoons pure vanilla extract

Cake Variation

Banana Chocolate Chip Split Cake (page 37)

1. Preheat the oven to 350°F (180°C). Grease and flour three 8-inch round cake pans and line with parchment circles.

2. In the bowl of a stand mixer fitted with the paddle attachment, combine the flour, sugar, cinnamon, baking soda, baking powder and salt. Mix on low speed until blended.

3. In a medium bowl, combine the mashed banana, milk, sour cream, vegetable oil, melted butter, hot water, eggs and vanilla. Pour into the bowl with the dry ingredients and mix on low speed until combined. Stop the mixer and scrape down the sides and bottom of the bowl with a rubber spatula, then beat again on medium speed for 30 seconds.

4. Divide the batter evenly among the prepared cake pans and bake for 25 to 30 minutes, until a toothpick inserted in the centre of the cakes comes out clean. Allow the cakes to cool in their pans for 20 minutes before turning them out onto a wire rack. Remove the parchment paper from the bottom of each cake, turn them right side up and leave them to cool completely.

5. Cake layers will keep at cool room temperature, wrapped tightly in plastic wrap, for up to 24 hours.

Glorious Gingerbread Cake

Nothing reminds me of the holidays more than the smell of gingerbread baking in the oven. This moist holiday treat can be frosted to perfection with Cream Cheese Frosting (page 191) but also pairs well with a simple Bake Shop Vanilla Frosting (page 190)—topped with sprinkles, of course!

Makes two 8-inch round cakes

Unsalted butter, for greasing pans

3 cups (345 g) cake flour, sifted, plus more for pans

2 cups (400 g) granulated sugar

2 teaspoons ground ginger

1 teaspoon cinnamon

2 teaspoons baking soda

1 teaspoon baking powder

1 teaspoon salt

1 cup buttermilk, room temperature

½ cup vegetable oil

½ cup sour cream

½ cup hot water

⅓ cup molasses

2 large eggs, room temperature

2 teaspoons pure vanilla extract

1 teaspoon white vinegar

Cake Variation

Pastel Gingerbread Cake (page 50)

Cupcake Variation

Holiday Gingerbread Cupcakes (page 78)

1. Preheat the oven to 350°F (180°). Grease and flour two 8-inch round cake pans and line with parchment circles.

2. In the bowl of a stand mixer fitted with the paddle attachment, combine the flour, sugar, ginger, cinnamon, baking soda, baking powder and salt. Mix on low speed until blended, about 20 seconds.

3. In a small bowl, combine the buttermilk, vegetable oil, sour cream, hot water, molasses, eggs, vanilla and vinegar. Pour into the bowl with the dry ingredients and mix on low speed until just combined. Turn the mixer up to medium speed and beat for 30 seconds. Stop the mixer and scrape down the sides and bottom of the bowl with a rubber spatula, then beat again on medium speed for an additional 30 seconds.

4. Divide the batter evenly between the prepared pans and bake for 30 to 35 minutes, until a toothpick inserted in the centre of the cakes comes out clean. Allow the cakes to cool in their pans for 20 minutes before turning them out onto a wire rack. Remove the parchment paper from the bottom of each cake, turn them right side up and leave them to cool completely.

5. Cake layers will keep at cool room temperature, wrapped tightly in plastic wrap, for up to 24 hours.

Moist Red Velvet Cake

As a baker, I'm a little ashamed to admit that the first time I tried a red velvet cupcake was only a few years ago. I was on vacation and had a serious craving for cream cheese frosting, so when I stumbled upon a little bakery, I marched inside and ordered a red velvet cupcake—and instantly fell in love. In my opinion, my sweet and tangy Cream Cheese Frosting (page 191) is the only frosting that should ever coat a red velvet cake.

Makes two 8-inch round cake layers

Unsalted butter, for greasing pans

3 cups (345 g) cake flour, sifted, plus more for pans

2 cups (400 g) granulated sugar

3 tablespoons (20 g) Dutch-processed cocoa powder

2 teaspoons baking soda

1 teaspoon baking powder

½ teaspoon salt

1¼ cups buttermilk, room temperature

½ cup vegetable oil

½ cup sour cream

½ cup hot water

¼ cup red liquid food colouring (no-taste, if possible)

2 large eggs, room temperature

2 teaspoons pure vanilla extract

1 teaspoon white vinegar

Cake Variation

Red Velvet Oreo Sprinkle Cake (page 32)

1. Preheat the oven to 325°F (160°C). Grease and flour two 8-inch round cake pans and line with parchment circles.

2. In the bowl of a stand mixer fitted with the paddle attachment, combine the flour, sugar, cocoa powder, baking soda, baking powder and salt. Mix on low speed until blended, about 20 seconds.

3. In a small bowl, combine the buttermilk, vegetable oil, sour cream, hot water, food colouring, eggs, vanilla and vinegar. Pour into the bowl with the dry ingredients and mix on low speed until just combined. Turn the mixer up to medium speed and beat for 30 seconds. Stop the mixer and scrape down the sides and bottom of the bowl with a rubber spatula, then beat again on medium speed for an additional 30 seconds.

4. Divide the batter evenly between the prepared pans and bake for 30 to 35 minutes, until a toothpick inserted in the centre of the cakes comes out clean. Allow the cakes to cool in their pans for 20 minutes before turning them out onto a wire rack. Remove the parchment paper from the bottom of each cake, turn them right side up and leave them to cool completely.

5. Cake layers will keep at cool room temperature, wrapped tightly in plastic wrap, for up to 24 hours.

Vanilla Birthday Cake

This is, hands down, my favourite recipe in this book. I've always been a lover of vanilla cake—it's my go-to dessert every time I have a sugar craving. The buttermilk lends a hint of flavour while simultaneously adding moisture, and the vanilla frosting is the perfect sweet finish. Decorate with sprinkles, light some candles and dig in!

Makes one 8-inch round 3-layer cake; Serves 10 to 12

1 batch Dreamy Vanilla Cake (page 19)

2 batches Bake Shop Vanilla Frosting (page 190)

2 to 3 drops pink gel food colouring

Pastel sprinkles, for decorating

1. Make the Dreamy Vanilla Cake. Allow the cakes to cool completely.

2. While the cakes are cooling, make the Bake Shop Vanilla Frosting. Stir in the food colouring until blended, then place 2 cups of the frosting in a small bowl and set aside for piping the border.

3. Once the cakes have cooled completely, use a serrated knife to level each one, removing any domed top that may have formed (see instructions on page 14).

4. Place a nonslip square in the centre of a cake turntable and set a cake board on top. Apply a small dollop of the frosting to the centre of the cake board, and then place the first cake layer, cut side up, on top. Spread an even layer of frosting on the cake layer. Place the next cake layer, cut side up, on top and spread another even layer of frosting over it. Place the final cake layer, cut side down, on top, pressing down gently to help the layers stick together.

5. Use some of the frosting to crumb coat the whole cake (see instructions on page 15). Lift the cake off the turntable and transfer it to the refrigerator to set, about 30 minutes.

6. Once the cake has set, place it back on the turntable or on a cake plate. Use an offset spatula to apply the rest of the frosting to the cake, working from the top of the cake down and smoothing with a cake scraper (see instructions on page 15).

7. Fit a pastry bag with a large piping tip and fill with the remaining frosting. Pipe a border around the top and bottom of the cake. Add sprinkles to the border, if desired.

8. Serve immediately or store in the refrigerator for up to 24 hours. Allow the cake to stand at room temperature for at least 3 hours before serving.

Chocolate Sprinkle Cake

Chocolate, chocolate and more chocolate! From top to bottom, this decadent cake is the perfect dessert for anyone with a serious sweet tooth. For extra sweetness, serve with a scoop of Easy Macaron Ice Cream (page 147).

Makes one 8-inch round 3-layer cake; Serves 10 to 12

1 batch Ultimate Chocolate Cake (page 20)

2 batches Bake Shop Vanilla Frosting, chocolate variation (page 190)

Rainbow sprinkles, for decorating

1. Make the Ultimate Chocolate Cake. Allow the cakes to cool completely.

2. While the cakes are cooling, make the Chocolate Frosting. Place 2 cups of frosting in a small bowl and set aside for piping the border.

3. Once the cakes have cooled completely, use a serrated knife to level each one, removing any domed top that may have formed (see instructions on page 14).

4. Place a nonslip square in the centre of a cake turntable and set a cake board on top. Apply a small dollop of the frosting to the centre of the cake board, and then place the first cake layer, cut side up, on top. Spread an even layer of frosting on the cake layer. Place the next cake layer, cut side up, on top and spread another even layer of frosting over it. Place the final cake layer, cut side down, on top, pressing down gently to help the layers stick together.

5. Use some of the frosting to crumb coat the whole cake (see instructions on page 15). Lift the cake off the turntable and transfer it to the refrigerator to set, about 30 minutes.

6. Once the cake has set, place it back on the turntable or on a cake plate. Use an offset spatula to apply the rest of the frosting to the cake, working from the top of the cake down and smoothing with a cake scraper (see instructions on page 15).

7. Fit a pastry bag with a large piping tip and fill with the reserved frosting. Pipe a border around the top and bottom of the cake. Top with sprinkles.

8. Serve immediately or store in the refrigerator for up to 24 hours. Allow the cake to stand at room temperature for at least 2 hours before serving.

Red Velvet Oreo Sprinkle Cake

Sprinkled and packed full of cookie goodness, this cake is ready to party. Be sure to have larger plates on hand for serving, as these cake slices are sky-high!

Makes one 6-inch round 4-layer cake; Serves 8 to 10

1 batch Moist Red Velvet Cake batter (page 27)

1 batch Cream Cheese Frosting (page 191), divided

2 to 3 drops pink gel food colouring

¾ cup rainbow sprinkles (use jimmies for this recipe)

1 ¼ cups (about 8 cookies) roughly broken Oreos

1. Preheat the oven to 325°F (160°C). Grease and flour four 6-inch round cake pans and line with parchment circles.

2. Make the Moist Red Velvet Cake batter (steps 2 and 3). Divide the batter evenly among the prepared pans and bake for 30 to 35 minutes, until a toothpick inserted in the centre of the cakes comes out clean. Allow the cakes to cool in their pans for 15 minutes before turning them out onto a wire rack. Remove the parchment paper from the bottom of each cake, turn them right side up and leave them to cool completely.

3. While the cakes are cooling, make the Cream Cheese Frosting. Place 1½ cups of frosting in a small bowl, add the pink food colouring and mix with a rubber spatula until blended. Fold the sprinkles into the remaining frosting.

4. Once the cakes have cooled completely, use a serrated knife to level each one, removing any domed top that may have formed (see instructions on page 14).

5. Place a nonslip square in the centre of a cake turntable and set a cake board on top. Apply a small dollop of the sprinkle frosting to the centre of the cake board, and then place the first cake layer, cut side up, on top. Spread an even layer of the sprinkle frosting on the cake layer, then lightly press one-third of the broken Oreos into the frosting. Place the next cake layer, cut side up, on top and spread another even layer of sprinkle frosting over it, then press a third of the crushed Oreos into the frosting. Place the third cake layer, cut side up, on top and spread another even layer of sprinkle frosting over it, then press the remaining crushed Oreos into the frosting. Place the final cake layer, cut side down, on top, pressing down gently to help the layers stick together.

6. Use some of the sprinkle frosting to crumb coat the whole cake (see instructions on page 15). Lift the cake off of the turntable and transfer it to the refrigerator to set, about 30 minutes.

7. Once the cake has set, place it back on the turntable or on a cake plate. Use an offset spatula to apply the rest of the sprinkle frosting to the cake, working from the top of the cake down, smoothing with a cake scraper (see instructions on page 15). Once the cake is smooth, fit a pastry bag with a large piping tip and half fill with the pink frosting. Pipe a border around the top and bottom of the cake.

8. Serve immediately or store in the refrigerator for up to 24 hours. Allow the cake to stand at room temperature for at least 2 hours before serving.

Cookie Dough Chocolate Sprinkle Cake

Stuffed with loads of cookie dough, this cake quickly became a favourite among my friends. Its pretty pastel exterior and drippy chocolate ganache topping make this cake one that will please almost any dessert lover.

Makes one 8-inch round 3-layer cake; Serves 10 to 12

1 batch Ultimate Chocolate Cake (page 20)

1 batch Eggless Chocolate Chip Cookie Dough (page 197)

1 batch Bake Shop Vanilla Frosting (page 190), divided

1 to 2 drops blue gel paste food colouring

2 to 3 drops turquoise gel paste food colouring

1 batch Chocolate Ganache (page 196)

Pastel sprinkles, for decorating

1. Make the Ultimate Chocolate Cake. Allow the cakes to cool completely.

2. While the cakes are cooling, make the Eggless Chocolate Chip Cookie Dough.

3. Make the Bake Shop Vanilla Frosting. Add the blue and turquoise food colouring and beat on medium speed to blend. Place ½ cup of frosting in a small bowl and set aside for decorating.

4. Once the cakes have cooled completely, use a serrated knife to level each one, removing any domed top that may have formed (see instructions on page 14).

5. Place a nonslip square in the centre of a cake turntable and set a cake board on top. Apply a dollop of frosting to the centre of the cake board, and then place the first cake layer, cut side up, on top. Spread half of the cookie dough on the cake layer. Place the next cake layer, cut side up, on top and spread the other half of the cookie dough over it. Place the final cake layer, cut side down, on top, pressing down gently to help the layers stick together. Run an offset spatula around the cake to remove any excess cookie dough.

6. Use some of the frosting to crumb coat the whole cake (see instructions on page 15). Lift the cake off the turntable and transfer it to the refrigerator to set, about 30 minutes.

7. Once the cake has set, place it back on the turntable. Use an offset spatula to apply the reserved ½ cup of frosting to the cake, working from the top of the cake down and smoothing with a cake scraper (see instructions on page 15). Place back in the refrigerator to set for 20 minutes.

8. Make the Chocolate Ganache and set aside to cool.

9. Once the cake has set, place it back on the turntable. Carefully pour the ganache onto the top of the cake, then use an offset spatula to smooth it out towards the edges, slowly turning the turntable at the same time. Top with sprinkles.

10. Serve immediately or store in the refrigerator for up to 24 hours. Allow the cake to stand at room temperature for at least 2 hours before serving.

Banana Chocolate Chip Split Cake

This sweet treat is the cake version of the famous banana split dessert. For extra decadence, serve with a spoonful of Vanilla Bean Whipped Cream (page 199) and some toasted nuts.

Makes one 8-inch round 3-layer cake; Serves 10 to 12

1 batch Best Banana Cake batter (page 23)

1 cup (175 g) semi-sweet chocolate chips

1 teaspoon cake flour, for the chocolate chips

2 batches Cream Cheese Frosting (page 191), divided

1 to 2 drops pink gel food colouring

1 batch Chocolate Ganache (page 196)

10 to 12 maraschino cherries, for decorating

1. Preheat the oven to 350°F (180°C). Grease and flour three 8-inch round cake pans and line with parchment circles.

2. Make the Best Banana Cake batter (steps 2 and 3). In a small bowl, toss the chocolate chips with the flour until coated. This will keep them from sinking to the bottom of the cakes while they bake. Fold the chocolate chips into the batter with a rubber spatula.

3. Divide the batter evenly among the prepared pans and bake for 25 to 30 minutes, until a toothpick inserted in the centre of the cakes comes out clean. Allow the cakes to cool in their pans for 20 minutes before turning them out onto a wire rack. Remove the parchment paper from the bottom of each cake and leave them to cool completely.

4. While the cakes are cooling, make the Cream Cheese Frosting. Place 1 cup of frosting in a small bowl, cover with plastic wrap and set aside for decorating.

5. Once the cakes have cooled completely, use a serrated knife to level each one, removing any domed top that may have formed (see instructions on page 14).

6. Place a nonslip square in the centre of a cake turntable and set a cake board on top. Apply a small dollop of the frosting to the centre of the cake board, and then place the first cake layer, cut side up, on top. Spread an even layer of frosting on the cake layer. Place the next cake layer, cut side up, on top and spread another even layer of frosting over it. Place the final cake layer, cut side down, on top, pressing down gently to help the layers stick together.

7. Use some of the frosting to crumb coat the whole cake (see instructions on page 15). Lift the cake off the turntable and transfer it to the refrigerator to set, about 30 minutes.

8. While the cake is setting, add the pink food colouring to the remaining frosting and mix with a rubber spatula to blend. Once the cake has set, place it back on the cake turntable. Use an offset spatula to apply the pink frosting to the cake, working from the top of the cake down and smoothing with a cake scraper (see instructions on page 15). Use a decorating comb to create texture around the cake, then place the cake back in the refrigerator to set, about 30 minutes.

9. While the cake is setting, make the Chocolate Ganache and allow to cool completely. Once the cake has set, place it back on the cake turntable. Carefully pour the ganache onto the top of the cake, then use an offset spatula to smooth it out towards the edges, slowly turning the turntable at the same time.

10. Unwrap the small bowl of white frosting. Using a small ice cream scoop or a spoon, apply scoops of the frosting around the top of the cake. Top each scoop with a cherry.

11. Serve immediately or store in the refrigerator for up to 24 hours. Allow the cake to stand at room temperature for at least 2 hours before serving.

Summer Party Cake

I came up with the idea for this cake when I found myself with broken cookies that I couldn't sell but didn't want to throw away. My Summertime S'more Cupcakes (page 68) were extremely popular, so I thought that combining chocolate cake layers with cookies, plus a sweet frosting, all wrapped up in toasty marshmallow just might be delicious. Inspired by evenings spent sitting around campfires, this quickly became one of my most requested cakes.

Makes one 8-inch round 3-layer cake; Serves 10 to 12

1 batch Brown Butter S'more Sandwich Cookies (page 104), without the fillings

1 batch Ultimate Chocolate Cake (page 20)

1 batch Bake Shop Vanilla Frosting, caramel variation (page 190)

2 batches Dreamy Marshmallow Frosting (page 192)

1. Make the Brown Butter cookies (steps 1 through 7). Allow the cookies to cool completely. Once cooled, place the cookies in a resealable plastic bag and use a rolling pin to gently roll and crush the cookies into crumbs.

2. Make the Ultimate Chocolate Cake. Allow the cakes to cool completely.

3. While the cakes are cooling, make the Caramel Frosting and set aside.

4. Once the cakes have cooled completely, use a serrated knife to level each one, removing any domed top that may have formed (see instructions on page 14).

5. Place a nonslip square in the centre of a cake turntable and set a cake board on top. Apply a small dollop of the frosting to the centre of the cake board, and then place the first cake layer, cut side up, on top. Spread an even layer of the frosting on the cake layer, then press half of the cookie crumbs into the frosting. Place the next cake layer, cut side up, on top and spread another even layer of frosting over it, then press the remaining cookie crumbs into the frosting. Place the final cake layer, cut side down, on top, pressing down gently to help the layers stick together.

6. Use some of the frosting to crumb coat the whole cake (see instructions on page 15). Lift the cake off the turntable and transfer it to the refrigerator to set, about 30 minutes.

7. While the cake is setting, make the Dreamy Marshmallow Frosting. Once the cake has set, place it back on the cake turntable or on a heatproof plate. Use an offset spatula to apply the frosting to the cake, working from the top of the cake down and smoothing with a cake scraper (see instructions on page 15). Run a decorating comb around the cake to create texture. Fit a pastry bag with a large piping tip and fill with the remaining marshmallow frosting. Pipe dollops on top of the cake.

8. Using a kitchen torch, carefully brown the frosting on the top and sides of the cake, moving the flame back and forth gently to avoid burning the frosting.

9. Serve immediately or store in the refrigerator for up to 24 hours. Allow the cake to stand at room temperature for at least 2 hours before serving.

Chocolate Raspberry Truffle Cake

This sinful cake was made for serious chocolate cravings. Fresh raspberries help to balance out the chocolate's sweetness—a classic combination!

Makes one 6-inch round 3-layer cake; Serves 8 to 10

CAKE

Unsalted butter, for greasing pans

1¾ cups plus 2 tablespoons (235 g) all-purpose flour, plus more for pans

1½ cups (300 g) granulated sugar

1 cup (110 g) Dutch-processed cocoa powder

1 teaspoon baking soda

½ teaspoon baking powder

½ teaspoon salt

¼ cup (45 g) semi-sweet chocolate chips

1½ cups whole milk, room temperature

½ cup vegetable oil

¼ cup sour cream

1 large egg, room temperature

1 teaspoon pure vanilla extract

FOR FROSTING AND DECORATING

2 batches Chocolate Ganache (page 196)

1 batch Bake Shop Vanilla Frosting, chocolate variation (page 190)

1 cup fresh raspberries, washed and dried thoroughly, plus more for decorating

1. Preheat the oven to 350°F (180°C). Grease and flour three 6-inch round cake pans and line with parchment circles.

2. In the bowl of a stand mixer fitted with the paddle attachment, combine the flour, sugar, cocoa powder, baking soda, baking powder and salt. Mix on low speed until blended.

3. In a heatproof bowl set over a saucepan of simmering water, melt the chocolate chips, stirring often with a rubber spatula to prevent burning. Remove the bowl from the pan and set aside.

4. In a medium bowl, whisk together the milk, vegetable oil, sour cream, egg and vanilla. Pour the mixture into the bowl with the dry ingredients, then add the melted chocolate. Mix on low speed until the mixture comes together, then turn up to medium speed and beat for about 30 seconds. Stop the mixer and scrape down the sides and bottom of the bowl with a rubber spatula, then beat again on medium speed for an additional 10 seconds.

5. Divide the batter evenly among the prepared cake pans. Bake for 27 to 30 minutes, until a toothpick inserted in the centre of the cakes comes out clean. Allow the cakes to cool in their pans for 15 minutes before turning them out onto a wire rack. Remove the parchment paper from the bottom of each cake and leave them to cool completely.

6. While the cakes are cooling, make the Chocolate Ganache. Set aside to cool.

7. Make the Chocolate Frosting. Fit a pastry bag with a plain piping tip and half fill with the frosting. Set aside.

8. Once the cakes have cooled completely, use a serrated knife to level each one, removing any domed top that may have formed (see instructions on page 14).

9. Place a nonslip square in the centre of a cake turntable and set a cake board on top. Apply a small dollop of the frosting to the centre of the cake board, and then place the first cake layer, cut side up, on top. Pipe a frosting border around the perimeter of the cake layer, then spoon some of the ganache into the middle. Gently press half of the raspberries into the ganache. Place the next cake layer, cut side up, on top. Pipe another frosting border around the perimeter, spoon more of the ganache into the middle and gently press the remaining raspberries into the ganache. Place the final cake layer, cut side down, on top, pressing down gently to help the layers stick together.

10. Use some of the frosting to crumb coat the whole cake (see instructions on page 15). Lift the cake off the turntable and transfer it to the refrigerator to set, about 30 minutes.

11. Once the cake has set, place it back on the cake turntable or on a cake plate. Use an offset spatula to apply the rest of the frosting to the cake, working from the top of the cake down and smoothing with a cake scraper (see instructions on page 15). Once the cake is smooth, use a decorating comb to create a pattern around the cake, then place the cake back in the refrigerator to set, about 30 minutes.

12. Once the cake has set, place it back on the cake turntable. Carefully pour the room-temperature ganache onto the top of the cake, then use an offset spatula to smooth it out towards the edges, slowly turning the turntable at the same time. Decorate with raspberries.

13. Serve immediately or store in the refrigerator for up to 24 hours. Allow the cake to stand at room temperature for at least 2 hours before serving.

Pink Coconut Mini Cakes

My friend's husband is obsessed with any dessert that has coconut in it, and a few years ago she asked me to bake him a birthday cake flavoured with—you guessed it—coconut. Since then, I've been in charge of baking his cakes, and every year I try something a little different. When my friend wanted him to have his very own cake that he could devour all on his own, I made him a mini version—with a matching one for her, too!

Makes two 4-inch round 3-layer cakes; Serves 2 to 4, each cake

CAKE

2½ cups (285 g) cake flour, sifted, plus more for pans

1¼ cups (250 g) granulated sugar

1 tablespoon baking powder

½ teaspoon salt

½ cup plus 1 tablespoon (120 g) unsalted butter, cut into pieces, room temperature, plus more for pans

¾ cup buttermilk, room temperature

3 tablespoons coconut extract, divided

1 teaspoon pure vanilla extract

2 large egg whites, room temperature

1 large egg, room temperature

3 tablespoons unsweetened shredded coconut

FOR FROSTING AND DECORATING

1 batch Bake Shop Vanilla Frosting (page 190)

1½ cups sweetened pink and white shredded coconut

2 maraschino cherries

1. Preheat the oven to 350°F (180°C). Grease and flour six 4-inch round cake pans and line with parchment circles.

2. In the bowl of a stand mixer fitted with the paddle attachment, combine the flour, sugar, baking powder and salt. Mix on low speed until blended. With the mixer running on low speed, add the butter, a few pieces at a time, mixing until the mixture is crumbly.

3. In a small bowl, whisk together the buttermilk, 1 tablespoon of the coconut extract and the vanilla. With the mixer running on low speed, pour two-thirds of the buttermilk mixture into the bowl with the dry ingredients and mix until the batter comes together. Turn the mixer up to medium speed and beat for about 90 seconds, until the batter has gained volume. Stop the mixer and scrape down the sides and bottom of the bowl with a rubber spatula.

4. Add the egg whites and egg to the remaining buttermilk mixture and whisk together with a fork. Pour half of the egg mixture into the mixer bowl and mix on low speed until some of the liquid has been incorporated, then beat on medium speed to combine completely, 15 to 20 seconds. Stop the mixer, add the remaining egg mixture and beat for an additional 15 seconds on medium speed. Fold in the coconut with a rubber spatula.

5. Divide the batter evenly among the prepared pans and bake for 17 to 22 minutes, until a toothpick inserted in the centre of the cakes comes out clean. Allow the cakes to cool in their pans for about 10 minutes before turning them out onto a wire rack. Remove the parchment paper from the bottom of each cake and leave them to cool completely.

6. While the cakes are cooling, make the Bake Shop Vanilla Frosting. Stir in the remaining 2 tablespoons of coconut extract.

7. Once the cakes have cooled completely, use a serrated knife to level each one, removing any domed top that may have formed (see instructions on page 14).

8. Place a nonslip square in the centre of a cake turntable and set a cake board on top. Apply a small dollop of the frosting to the centre of the cake board, and then place the first cake layer, cut side up, on top. Spread an even layer of frosting on the cake layer. Place the next cake layer, cut side up, on top and spread another even layer of frosting over it. Place the final cake layer, cut side down, on top, pressing down gently to help the layers stick together.

9. Use some of the frosting to crumb coat the whole cake (see instructions on page 15). Lift the cake off the turntable and transfer it to the refrigerator to set, about 30 minutes. Repeat with the remaining cake layers.

10. Once the cakes have set, place one of them back on the cake turntable. Use an offset spatula to apply about half of the remaining frosting to the cake, working from the top of the cake down and smoothing with a cake scraper (see instructions on page 15). Repeat with the second cake.

11. Divide the shredded coconut into two bowls. Using your hand, scoop up some of the coconut from the first bowl and gently toss it onto the top and sides of the cake, working your way around until it is completely covered. Repeat with the remaining cake. Top each cake with a maraschino cherry.

12. Serve immediately or store in the refrigerator for up to 24 hours. Allow the cakes to stand at room temperature for at least 2 hours before serving.

Lemon Blueberry Cake

Light, lemony layers paired with fresh blueberries and a tart, creamy frosting—the perfect cake to serve on warm summer nights. Eat the cake by itself or whip up a batch of Vanilla Bean Whipped Cream (page 199) to accompany it.

Makes one 8-inch round 3-layer cake; Serves 10 to 12

1 batch Dreamy Vanilla Cake batter (page 19)

1 tablespoon lemon extract

Zest of 1 lemon

1½ cups fresh blueberries

2 tablespoons cake flour, for the blueberries

2 batches Cream Cheese Frosting, lemon variation (page 191)

White sprinkles, for decorating

1. Preheat the oven to 350°F (180°C). Grease and flour three 8-inch round cake pans and line with parchment circles.

2. Make the Dreamy Vanilla Cake batter (steps 2 through 4). Once the batter comes together after you've added the eggs, stir in the lemon extract and lemon zest. In a small bowl, toss the blueberries with the flour until coated, then fold into the batter with a rubber spatula.

3. Divide the batter evenly among the prepared pans and bake for 23 to 27 minutes, until a toothpick inserted in the centre of the cakes comes out clean. Allow the cakes to cool in their pans for 15 minutes before turning them out onto a wire rack. Remove the parchment paper from the bottom of each cake and leave them to cool completely.

4. While the cakes are cooling, make the Lemon Cream Cheese Frosting. Once the cakes have cooled completely, use a serrated knife to level each one, removing any domed top that may have formed (see instructions on page 14).

5. Place a nonslip square in the centre of a cake turntable and set a cake board on top. Apply a small dollop of the frosting to the centre of the cake board, and then place the first cake layer, cut side up, on top. Spread an even layer of frosting on the cake layer and then place the next cake layer, cut side up, on top.

Spread another even layer of frosting over the cake layer. Place the final cake layer, cut side down, on top, pressing down gently to help the layers stick together. Use some of the frosting to crumb coat the whole cake (see instructions on page 15). Lift the cake off the turntable and transfer it to the refrigerator to set, about 30 minutes.

6. Once the cake has set, place it back on the cake turntable. Use an offset spatula to apply the rest of the frosting to the cake, working from the top of the cake down and smoothing with a cake scraper. Top with sprinkles.

7. Serve immediately or store in the refrigerator for up to 24 hours. Allow the cake to stand at room temperature for at least 2 hours before serving.

Pastel Gingerbread Cake

This pastel cake is sure to impress. The watercolour design makes it look like you spent hours painting it, but all it takes is tinted frosting and a little smoothing practice!

Makes one 6-inch round 4-layer cake; Serves 8 to 10

1 batch Glorious Gingerbread Cake batter (page 24)

1 batch Cream Cheese Frosting (page 191)

1 drop pink gel food colouring

1 drop purple gel food colouring

White sprinkles, for decorating

Edible glitter, for decorating (I use CK)

1. Preheat the oven to 350°F (180°C). Grease and flour four 6-inch round cake pans. Line with parchment circles.

2. Make the Glorious Gingerbread Cake batter (steps 2 and 3). Divide the batter evenly among the prepared pans and bake for 30 to 35 minutes, until a toothpick inserted in the centre of the cakes comes out clean. Allow the cakes to cool in their pans for 15 minutes before turning them out onto a wire rack. Remove the parchment paper from the bottom of each cake and leave them to cool completely.

3. While the cakes are cooling, make the Cream Cheese Frosting. Scoop 2 tablespoons of frosting into a small bowl, add the pink food colouring and mix with a spoon to blend. Scoop 2 more tablespoons of frosting into another small bowl, add the purple food colouring and mix with a spoon to blend. Cover the bowls with plastic wrap and set aside.

4. Once the cakes have cooled completely, use a serrated knife to level each one, removing any domed top that may have formed (see instructions on page 14).

5. Place a nonslip square in the centre of a cake turntable and set a cake board on top. Apply a small dollop of the frosting to the centre of the cake board, and then place the first cake layer, cut side up, on top. Spread an even layer of frosting on the cake layer. Place the next cake layer, cut side up, on top and spread another even layer of frosting over it. Place the third cake layer, cut side up, on top and spread another even layer of frosting over it. Place the final cake layer, cut side down, on top, pressing down gently to help the layers stick together.

6. Use some of the frosting to crumb coat the whole cake (see instructions on page 15). Lift the cake off the turntable and transfer it to the refrigerator to set, about 30 minutes.

7. Once the cake has set, place it back on the cake turntable. Use an offset spatula to apply the rest of the white frosting to the cake working from the top of the cake down and smoothing with a cake scraper (see instructions on page 15).

8. Once the cake is smooth, use a spoon to gently apply dollops of pink and purple frosting all around the cake, then smooth over with a cake scraper, creating a watercolour effect. Top with sprinkles and edible glitter.

9. Serve immediately or store in the refrigerator for up to 24 hours. Allow the cake to stand at room temperature for at least 2 hours before serving.

Cinnamon Swirl Cake

This swirly-layered cake is sure to delight anyone with a love for cinnamon buns. Serve as an after-breakfast treat or just skip right past breakfast and dive straight into dessert.

Makes one 6-inch round 3-layer cake; Serves 8 to 10

CAKE

3 cups (345 g) cake flour, sifted, plus more for pans

1 ½ cups (300 g) granulated sugar

1 tablespoon baking powder

½ teaspoon salt

½ cup plus 2 tablespoons (130 g) unsalted butter, cut into pieces, room temperature, plus more for pans

1 cup plus 2 tablespoons buttermilk, room temperature

2 teaspoons pure vanilla extract

3 large egg whites, room temperature

2 large eggs, room temperature

2 tablespoons cinnamon

FOR FROSTING AND DECORATING

1 batch Cream Cheese Frosting (page 191)

White sprinkles (optional)

1. Preheat the oven to 350°F (180°C). Grease and flour three 6-inch round cake pans and line with parchment circles.

2. In the bowl of a stand mixer fitted with the paddle attachment, combine the flour, sugar, baking powder and salt. Mix on low speed until blended. With the mixer running on low speed, add the butter, a few pieces at a time, mixing until the mixture is crumbly.

3. In a small bowl, whisk together the buttermilk and vanilla. With the mixer running on low speed, pour two-thirds of the buttermilk mixture into the bowl with the dry ingredients and mix until the batter comes together. Turn the mixer up to medium speed and beat for about 90 seconds, until the batter has gained volume. Stop the mixer and scrape down the sides and bottom of the bowl with a rubber spatula.

4. Add the egg whites and egg to the remaining buttermilk mixture and whisk together with a fork. Pour half of the egg mixture into the mixer bowl and mix on low speed until some of the liquid has been incorporated, then beat on medium speed to combine completely, 15 to 20 seconds. Stop the mixer, add the remaining egg mixture and beat for an additional 15 seconds on medium speed.

5. Scoop ½ cup of batter into a small bowl. Add the cinnamon and stir together with a spoon until blended. Divide the remaining batter evenly among the prepared pans, then distribute an even amount of the cinnamon batter over each pan. Use the handle of a spoon to swirl the two batters together, creating a marbled effect.

6. Bake for 24 to 28 minutes, until a toothpick inserted in the centre of the cakes comes out clean. Allow the cakes to cool in their pans for about 20 minutes before turning them out onto a wire rack. Remove the parchment paper from the bottom of each cake and leave them to cool completely.

7. While the cakes are cooling, make the Cream Cheese Frosting. Once the cakes have cooled completely, use a serrated knife to level each one, removing any domed top that may have formed (see instructions on page 14).

8. Place a nonslip square in the centre of a cake turntable and set a cake board on top. Apply a small dollop of the frosting to the centre of the cake board, and then place the first cake layer, cut side up, on top. Spread an even layer of frosting on the cake layer. Place the next cake layer, cut side up, on top and spread another even layer of frosting over it. Place the final cake layer, cut side down, on top, pressing down gently to help the layers stick together.

9. Use some of the frosting to crumb coat the whole cake (see instructions on page 15). Lift the cake off the turntable and transfer it to the refrigerator to set, about 30 minutes.

10. Once the cake has set, place it back on the cake turntable. Use an offset spatula to apply most of the frosting to the cake, working from the top of the cake down and smoothing with a cake scraper (see instructions on page 15).

11. Add sprinkles to the border, if desired.

12. Serve immediately or store in the refrigerator for up to 24 hours. Allow the cake to stand at room temperature for at least 3 hours before serving.

Cupcake Cravings

Sprinkly Vanilla Party Cupcakes

Nothing says "party" like confetti sprinkles, especially when they're baked right into cupcakes. Swirls of fluffy, sweet frosting and even more sprinkles make these cupcakes the perfect party-time treat.

Makes 24 cupcakes

1 batch Dreamy Vanilla Cake batter (page 19)

¾ cup confetti sequin sprinkles

1 batch Cake Batter Frosting (page 193)

Rainbow sprinkles, for decorating

1. Preheat the oven to 350°F (180°C) and position the racks in the centre of the oven. Line two cupcake pans with 24 cupcake liners.

2. Make the Dreamy Vanilla Cake batter (steps 2 through 4). Once the batter is ready, fold in the confetti sequin sprinkles with a rubber spatula.

3. Divide the batter evenly among the liners and bake for 18 to 20 minutes, until a toothpick inserted in the centre of the cupcakes comes out clean. Immediately remove the cupcakes from the cupcake pans and place on a wire rack to cool completely.

4. Make the Cake Batter Frosting. Fit a pastry bag with a large piping tip and half fill with the frosting. Pipe generous dollops onto the cupcakes. Use the back of a small spoon to move the frosting around, creating space for the sprinkles. Add sprinkles to each cupcake, being as generous as you like.

5. Cupcakes will keep in a container, covered loosely with plastic wrap, at room temperature, for up to 2 days.

French Cupcakes

In the early days of Sweet Bake Shop, I found myself struggling to figure out a use for the occasional macarons that were just a little bit too big to fit into their boxes. After all, they were perfectly good macarons, and throwing them away would be tragic. One day, I decided to put a few on top of my vanilla cupcakes and see how customers reacted to this unusual combination. The response was overwhelmingly positive, and French Cupcakes were added to my menu. In truth, there is nothing particularly "French" about these cupcakes—except for the French macaron that crowns each one.

Makes 24 cupcakes

24 macarons of your choice (pages 168 to 185), made ahead

1 batch Dreamy Vanilla Cake batter (page 19)

1 batch Bake Shop Vanilla Frosting (page 190)

1. Preheat the oven to 350°F (180°C) and position the racks in the centre of the oven. Line two cupcake pans with 24 cupcake liners.

2. Make the Dreamy Vanilla Cake batter (steps 2 through 4). Divide the batter evenly among the liners and bake for 18 to 20 minutes, until a toothpick inserted into the centre of the cupcakes comes out clean. Immediately remove the cupcakes from the cupcake pans and place on a wire rack to cool completely.

3. Make the Bake Shop Vanilla Frosting. Fit a pastry bag with a piping tip and half fill with the frosting. Pipe small swirls onto each cupcake, beginning in the middle and swirling up and out. Place a macaron on top of each swirl of frosting, pressing down gently to help it stick in place.

4. Cupcakes will keep in a container, covered loosely with plastic wrap, at room temperature, for up to 2 days.

Vegan Vanilla Cupcakes

I've had so many less-than-amazing vegan desserts over the years that I've been put off by them. Or at least, I was. Strolling the streets of London while on vacation, I came across a little bakery tucked away in a tiny alley off Carnaby Street. Its pastel-perfect exterior drew me in immediately, and I ordered a box of cupcakes to take away, two of which were a vegan vanilla flavour for my vegan friend who was with me. We sat outside on a bench and dove into our cupcakes, and I was absolutely shocked at how delicious and moist the vegan cupcakes were. I knew that I needed to create my own version as soon as possible. I started testing out recipes as soon as I got home, and these were the winners!

Makes 12 cupcakes

CUPCAKES

2 cups (230 g) cake flour, sifted

1 cup plus 2 tablespoons (225 g) granulated sugar

2½ teaspoons baking powder

½ cup (115 g) unsalted vegan butter, room temperature (I use Earth Balance)

¾ cup unsweetened dairy-free milk, room temperature (I use almond milk)

½ teaspoon pure vanilla extract

2 tablespoons powdered egg replacer

5 tablespoons warm water

2 tablespoons dairy-free yogurt (I use soy yogurt)

VEGAN VANILLA FROSTING

4 cups (500 g) confectioners' sugar

¼ cup (55 g) unsalted or lightly salted vegan butter, room temperature

3 to 5 tablespoons unsweetened dairy-free milk, cold (I use almond milk)

1 vanilla bean, seeds scraped (or 1 teaspoon pure vanilla extract)

Sprinkles, for decorating (optional)

1. Preheat the oven to 350°F (180°C). Line a cupcake pan with 12 cupcake liners.

2. In the bowl of a stand mixer fitted with the paddle attachment, combine the flour, sugar and baking powder. Mix on low speed until blended. With the mixer running on low speed, add the vegan butter, a few pieces at a time, mixing until the mixture is crumbly.

3. In a liquid measuring cup or small bowl, whisk together the dairy-free milk and vanilla. With the mixer running on low speed, pour two-thirds of the milk mixture into the bowl with the flour mixture and mix until the batter comes together. Turn the mixer up to medium speed and beat for about 90 seconds, until the batter has gained volume. Stop the mixer and scrape down the sides and bottom of the bowl with a rubber spatula.

4. To the remaining one-third of the milk mixture, add the egg replacer, warm water and dairy-free yogurt and whisk together with a fork until smooth. Pour half of the mixture into the mixer bowl and mix on low speed until some of the liquid has been incorporated, then beat on medium speed to combine completely, 15 to 20 seconds. Stop the mixer, add the remaining egg mixture and beat for an additional 15 seconds on medium speed.

5. Divide the batter evenly among the liners and bake for 18 to 20 minutes, until a toothpick inserted in the centre of the cupcakes comes out clean. Immediately remove the cupcakes from the cupcake pans and place on a wire rack to cool completely.

6. Make the Vegan Vanilla Frosting: In the bowl of a stand mixer fitted with the paddle attachment, combine the confectioners' sugar, vegan butter, dairy-free milk and vanilla. Mix on low speed until the mixture comes together, then turn the mixer up to medium speed and beat until light and creamy, about 5 minutes.

7. Use the back of a spoon or a small offset spatula to spread the frosting onto each cupcake, moving it right to the inside edges of the paper liner. Top with sprinkles, if desired.

8. Cupcakes will keep in a container, covered loosely with plastic wrap, at room temperature, for up to 2 days.

Double Chocolate Cupcakes

Sometimes a simple chocolate-on-chocolate cupcake is just what you're craving. Dress them up with sprinkles, gold leaf and meringues or just eat them as is—the choice is yours.

Makes 12 cupcakes

CUPCAKES

1¼ cups (160 g) all-purpose flour

1 cup (200 g) granulated sugar

¾ cup (85 g) Dutch-processed cocoa powder

1 teaspoon baking soda

½ teaspoon baking powder

½ teaspoon salt

3 tablespoons (35 g) semi-sweet chocolate chips

1 cup whole milk, room temperature

¼ cup sour cream

¼ cup vegetable oil

2 large eggs, room temperature

1 teaspoon pure vanilla extract

FOR FROSTING AND DECORATING

1 batch Vanilla Meringues (page 140)

1 batch Bake Shop Vanilla Frosting, chocolate variation (page 190)

Pastel sprinkles

Edible gold flakes (I use Cote D'Azur)

1. Make the Vanilla Meringues for the decoration. Allow them to cool completely. (Meringues can be made up to 2 weeks in advance.)

2. Make the cupcakes. Preheat the oven to 350°F (180°C). Line a cupcake pan with 12 cupcake liners.

3. In the bowl of a stand mixer fitted with the paddle attachment, combine the flour, sugar, cocoa powder, baking soda, baking powder and salt. Mix on low speed until blended.

4. In a heatproof bowl set over a saucepan of simmering water, melt the chocolate chips, stirring often with a rubber spatula to prevent burning. Remove the bowl from the pan and set aside to cool.

5. In a small bowl, whisk together the milk, sour cream, vegetable oil, eggs and vanilla. Pour the mixture into the bowl with the dry ingredients, add the melted chocolate and beat on medium speed for about 30 seconds. Stop the mixer and scrape down the sides and bottom of the bowl with a rubber spatula, then beat again on medium speed until well blended, about 10 seconds.

6. Divide the batter evenly among the liners and bake for 18 to 20 minutes, until a toothpick inserted in the centre of the cupcakes comes out clean. Immediately remove the cupcakes from the cupcake pan and place on a wire rack to cool completely.

7. Make the Chocolate Frosting. Fit a pastry bag with a large piping tip and half fill with the frosting. Pipe a swirl onto each cupcake. Top with sprinkles and gold flakes and finish with a meringue.

8. Cupcakes will keep in a container, covered loosely with plastic wrap, at room temperature, for up to 2 days.

Raspberry Ripple Cupcakes

These cupcakes taste just like the popular flavour of ice cream! Fresh raspberries, vanilla cake and vanilla frosting come together in a cupcake that reminds me of the frosty dessert that I love so very much.

Makes 12 cupcakes

CUPCAKES

2 cups plus 2 tablespoons (245 g) cake flour, sifted, plus more for the raspberries

1 cup plus 2 tablespoons (225 g) granulated sugar

2½ teaspoons baking powder

¼ teaspoon salt

½ cup (115 g) unsalted butter, cut into pieces, room temperature

¾ cup buttermilk, room temperature

2½ teaspoons pure vanilla extract

2 large egg whites, room temperature

1 large egg, room temperature

1 cup fresh raspberries

FOR FROSTING AND DECORATING

1 batch Bake Shop Vanilla Frosting (page 190)

1 cup fresh raspberries

White sprinkles

1. Preheat the oven to 350°F (180°C). Line a cupcake pan with 12 cupcake liners.

2. In the bowl of a stand mixer fitted with the paddle attachment, combine the flour, sugar, baking powder and salt. Mix on low speed until blended. With the mixer running on low speed, add the butter, a few pieces at a time, mixing until the mixture is crumbly.

3. In a liquid measuring cup or a small bowl, whisk together the buttermilk and vanilla. Pour two-thirds of the mixture into the bowl with the flour mixture and mix on low speed until the batter comes together. Turn the mixer up to medium speed and beat for about 90 seconds, until the batter has gained volume. Stop the mixer and scrape down the sides and bottom of the bowl with a rubber spatula.

4. Add the egg whites and the egg to the remaining buttermilk mixture and whisk together with a fork. Pour half of the egg mixture into the mixer bowl and beat on medium speed to combine, about 15 seconds. Stop the mixer, add the remaining egg mixture and beat for an additional 15 seconds on medium speed.

5. Place the raspberries in a small bowl and toss with 2 to 3 teaspoons of flour to coat. Fold them into the batter with a rubber spatula.

6. Divide the batter evenly among the liners and bake for 19 to 22 minutes, until a toothpick inserted in the centre of the cupcakes comes out clean (although a little berry juice is okay).

7. Allow the cupcakes to cool for about 5 minutes before removing them from the pan and placing on a wire rack to cool completely.

8. Make the Bake Shop Vanilla Frosting. Add the raspberries to the frosting and fold in with a rubber spatula.

9. Use an ice cream scoop to place generous scoops of frosting onto each cupcake. Top with sprinkles.

10. Cupcakes will keep in a container, covered loosely with plastic wrap, at room temperature, for up to 2 days.

Summertime S'more Cupcakes

If sitting around a campfire isn't for you (or simply isn't an option), that doesn't mean you have to miss out on marshmallowy, chocolaty goodness! Bring the outdoors in with these cupcakes, which combine chocolate, graham crackers and toasty marshmallow, all wrapped up neat and tidy in a paper liner.

Makes 12 cupcakes

CUPCAKES

1 cup graham cracker crumbs

¼ cup (55 g) unsalted butter, melted

1¼ cups (160 g) all-purpose flour

1 cup (200 g) granulated sugar

¾ cup (85 g) Dutch-processed cocoa powder

1 teaspoon baking soda

½ teaspoon baking powder

½ teaspoon salt

3 tablespoons (35 g) semi-sweet chocolate chips

1 cup whole milk, room temperature

¼ cup sour cream

¼ cup vegetable oil

2 large eggs, room temperature

1 teaspoon pure vanilla extract

FOR FROSTING

1 batch Chocolate Ganache (page 196)

2 batches Dreamy Marshmallow Frosting (page 192)

1. Preheat the oven to 350°F (180°F). Line a cupcake pan with 12 cupcake liners.

2. In a small bowl, combine the graham cracker crumbs and melted butter. Whisk together with a fork until completely combined. Divide the mixture evenly among liners, then press flat with the back of a tablespoon or your fingers. Bake for about 10 minutes, until the crumbs have just set. Remove from the oven and allow to cool.

3. In the bowl of a stand mixer fitted with the paddle attachment, combine the flour, sugar, cocoa powder, baking soda, baking powder and salt. Mix on low speed until blended.

4. In a heatproof bowl set over a saucepan of simmering water, melt the chocolate chips, stirring often with a rubber spatula to prevent burning. Remove the bowl from the pan and set aside to cool.

5. In a small bowl, whisk together the milk, sour cream, vegetable oil, eggs and vanilla. Pour the mixture into the bowl with the dry ingredients, add the melted chocolate and beat on medium speed for about 30 seconds. Stop the mixer and scrape down the sides and bottom of the bowl with a rubber spatula, then beat again on medium speed until well blended, about 10 seconds.

6. Divide the batter evenly among the liners and bake for 18 to 20 minutes, or until a toothpick inserted in the centre of the cupcakes comes out clean. Immediately remove the cupcakes from the cupcake pan and place on a wire rack to cool completely.

7. While the cupcakes are cooling, make the Chocolate Ganache. Allow it to cool slightly, making sure it stays just warm enough to be pourable.

8. Once the cupcakes have cooled, use a small, sharp knife or an apple corer to remove a small amount of cake from the middle of each cupcake, creating a well. Pour a small amount of the Chocolate Ganache into each hole, being careful to keep it from spilling over the top. Set aside.

9. Make the Dreamy Marshmallow Frosting. Fit a pastry bag with a large piping tip and half fill with the frosting. Pipe swirls on top of each cupcake, beginning in the middle and working your way up and out. Using a kitchen torch, carefully brown the frosting, moving the flame back and forth gently to avoid burning it.

10. Cupcakes will keep in a container, covered loosely with plastic wrap, at room temperature, for up to 2 days.

Carnival Caramel Popcorn Cupcakes

This moist chocolate cupcake topped with caramel frosting and caramel-drenched popcorn is a hit with both adults and kids alike. For an even sweeter experience, drizzle the frosting with Chocolate Ganache (page 196) before placing the popcorn on top.

Makes 24 cupcakes

1 batch Confetti Caramel Popcorn
(page 138)

1 batch Ultimate Chocolate Cake batter
(page 20)

1 batch Bake Shop Vanilla Frosting,
caramel variation (page 190)

1. Make the Confetti Caramel Popcorn and set aside.

2. Preheat the oven to 350°F (180°C) and position the racks in the centre of the oven. Line two cupcake pans with 24 cupcake liners.

3. Make the Ultimate Chocolate Cake batter (steps 2 through 4). Divide the batter evenly among the liners and bake for 18 to 22 minutes, until a toothpick inserted in the centre of the cupcakes comes out clean. Immediately remove the cupcakes from the cupcake pans and place on a wire rack to cool completely.

4. Make the Caramel Frosting. Fit a pastry bag with a large piping tip and half fill with the frosting. Pipe swirls onto each cupcake, then immediately top with the Confetti Caramel Popcorn.

5. Cupcakes will keep in a container, covered loosely with plastic wrap, at room temperature, for up to 2 days.

Vanilla Blackberry Crumble Cupcakes

Both my parents bake, and they each have their areas of expertise. My dad is the cakes and pies baker and my mom is the cookies and cheesecakes maker. My dad adds "a little of this and a handful of that," and my mom uses exact measurements. However, there is one thing that they both make, and it's my most requested dessert every time I go home to visit: blackberry crumble. It's always served warm with a scoop of vanilla ice cream, and leftovers are often eaten for breakfast the next morning. These cupcakes are a twist on that beloved dessert and are a customer favourite.

Makes 12 cupcakes

FILLINGS

1 batch Blackberry Compote (page 199)

1 batch Cookie Crumble (page 201)

CUPCAKES

2 cups plus 2 tablespoons (245 g) cake flour, sifted

1 cup plus 3 tablespoons (240 g) granulated sugar

2 teaspoons baking powder

½ teaspoon salt

½ cup (115 g) unsalted butter, cut into pieces, room temperature

¾ cup buttermilk, room temperature

1 tablespoon pure vanilla extract

2 large egg whites, room temperature

1 large egg, room temperature

FOR FROSTING AND DECORATING

1 batch Bake Shop Vanilla Frosting (page 190)

2 to 3 drops purple gel food colouring

White sprinkles

1. Make the Blackberry Compote and allow it to cool completely.

2. Make the Cookie Crumble and allow it to cool.

3. Preheat the oven to 350°F (180°C). Line a cupcake pan with 12 cupcake liners.

4. In the bowl of a stand mixer fitted with the paddle attachment, combine the flour, sugar, baking powder and salt. Mix on low speed until blended. With the mixer running on low speed, add the butter, a few pieces at a time, and mix on low speed until the mixture is crumbly.

5. In a small bowl, whisk together the buttermilk and vanilla. With the mixer running on low speed, pour two-thirds of the buttermilk mixture into the bowl with the dry ingredients and mix until the batter comes together. Turn the mixer up to medium speed and beat for about 90 seconds, until the batter has gained volume. Stop the mixer and scrape down the sides and bottom of the bowl with a rubber spatula.

6. Add the egg whites and egg to the remaining buttermilk mixture and whisk together with a fork. Pour half of the egg mixture into the mixer bowl and mix on low speed until some of the liquid has been incorporated, then beat on medium speed to combine completely, 15 to 20 seconds. Stop the mixer, add the remaining egg mixture and beat for an additional 15 seconds on medium speed.

7. Divide the batter evenly among the liners and bake for 18 to 20 minutes, until a toothpick inserted in the centre of the cupcakes comes out clean. Immediately remove the cupcakes from the cupcake pan and place on a wire rack to cool completely.

8. Once the cupcakes have cooled, use a small, sharp knife or an apple corer to remove a small amount of cake from the middle of each cupcake, creating a well. Carefully spoon some of the Blackberry Compote into each well, filling until just about full, then top with some of the cookie crumble.

9. Make the Bake Shop Vanilla Frosting. Scoop half of the frosting into a medium bowl, add the food colouring and mix with a spatula to blend. Fit a pastry bag with a large piping tip. Using a spatula, carefully scoop the white frosting into one side of the bag and the purple frosting into the other side, until the bag is half-full. Pipe swirls of frosting onto each cupcake. Top with sprinkles.

10. Cupcakes will keep in a container, covered loosely with plastic wrap, at room temperature, for up to 2 days.

Pink Lemonade Cupcakes

My absolute favourite drink as a child was pink lemonade. When we were kids, my best friend and I would mix up a batch, pour it into a plastic pitcher and sell it by the cup at our little roadside stand, where we also sold cookies and other sweets we'd made. These pink-tinted lemon cupcakes are inspired by those memories.

Makes 12 cupcakes

CUPCAKES

2¼ cups (260 g) cake flour, sifted

1 cup (200 g) granulated sugar

1 tablespoon baking powder

½ teaspoon salt

½ cup (115 g) unsalted butter, cut into pieces, room temperature

¾ cup buttermilk, room temperature

2 teaspoons lemon extract

1 teaspoon pure vanilla extract

Zest of 1 lemon

2 large egg whites, room temperature

1 large egg, room temperature

1 to 2 drops pink gel food colouring

FOR FROSTING AND DECORATING

1 batch Bake Shop Vanilla Frosting, pink lemonade variation (page 190)

White sprinkles

12 maraschino cherries

1. Preheat the oven to 350°F (180°C). Line a cupcake pan with 12 cupcake liners.

2. In the bowl of a stand mixer fitted with the paddle attachment, combine the flour, sugar, baking powder and salt. Mix on low speed until blended. With the mixer running on low speed, add the butter, piece by piece, mixing until the mixture is crumbly.

3. In a liquid measuring cup or a small bowl, whisk together the buttermilk, lemon and vanilla extracts and lemon zest. With the mixer running on low speed, pour two-thirds of the mixture into the bowl with the flour mixture and mix until the batter comes together. Turn the mixer up to medium speed and beat for about 90 seconds, until the batter has doubled in volume. Stop the mixer and scrape down the sides and bottom of the bowl with a rubber spatula.

4. Add the egg whites and the egg to the remaining buttermilk mixture and whisk together with a fork. Pour half of the mixture into the mixer bowl and beat on medium speed to combine, about 15 seconds. Stop the mixer, add the remaining egg mixture and beat for an additional 15 seconds on medium speed. Add the pink food colouring and beat to combine. Remove the bowl from the mixer and use a rubber spatula to give the batter one last mix, to ensure all the food colouring is blended in.

5. Divide the batter evenly among the liners and bake for 18 to 20 minutes, until a toothpick inserted in the centre of the cupcakes comes out clean. Immediately remove the cupcakes from the cupcake pan and place on a wire rack to cool completely.

6. Make the Pink Lemonade Frosting. Fit a pastry bag with a large piping tip and half fill with the frosting. Pipe swirls of frosting onto the cupcakes, then top with sprinkles and a cherry.

7. Cupcakes will keep in a container, covered loosely with plastic wrap, at room temperature, for up to 2 days.

Banana Caramel Supreme Cupcakes

These sticky-sweet and incredibly moist cupcakes bake up like a dream. Topped with swirls of caramel cream cheese frosting and drizzled with even more caramel, they are sure to be a crowd-pleaser at any party.

Makes 12 cupcakes

CUPCAKES

1 ¼ cups plus 2 tablespoons (160 g) cake flour, sifted

1 cup (200 g) granulated sugar

1 teaspoon cinnamon

1 teaspoon baking soda

½ teaspoon baking powder

½ teaspoon salt

¾ cup mashed ripe banana (about 2 medium bananas)

½ cup whole milk, room temperature

¼ cup sour cream

2 tablespoons unsalted butter, melted

2 tablespoons vegetable oil

1 large egg, room temperature

1 teaspoon pure vanilla extract

FOR FROSTING AND DECORATING

1 batch Wonderful Caramel (page 200)

1 batch Cream Cheese Frosting, caramel variation (page 191)

Rainbow sprinkles

1. Preheat the oven to 350°F (180°C). Line a cupcake pan with 12 cupcake liners.

2. In the bowl of a stand mixer fitted with the paddle attachment, combine the flour, sugar, cinnamon, baking soda, baking powder and salt. Mix on low speed until blended.

3. In a medium bowl, whisk together the mashed bananas, milk, sour cream, melted butter, vegetable oil, egg and vanilla. Pour into the bowl with the flour mixture and mix on low speed until combined. Stop the mixer and scrape down the sides and bottom of the bowl with a rubber spatula, then beat again on medium speed for 30 seconds.

4. Divide the batter evenly among the liners and bake for 18 to 20 minutes, until a toothpick inserted in the centre of the cupcakes comes out clean. Allow the cupcakes to cool for about 5 minutes before removing them from the pan and placing on a wire rack to cool completely.

5. Make the Wonderful Caramel and allow it to cool completely.

6. Make the Caramel Cream Cheese Frosting. Fit a pastry bag with a large piping tip and half fill with the frosting. Pipe swirls onto each cupcake. Use a spoon to drizzle caramel over the frosting swirls, then top with sprinkles.

7. Cupcakes will keep in a container, covered loosely with plastic wrap, at room temperature, for up to 2 days.

Holiday Gingerbread Cupcakes

The perfect treat to whip up during the holidays! These ultra-moist cupcakes are topped with a cinnamon cream cheese frosting, which balances out the sweetness of the cupcake. Finished with sprinkles and a pinch of edible glitter, they're party-ready.

Makes 24 cupcakes

1 batch Glorious Gingerbread Cake batter (page 24)

2 batches Cream Cheese Frosting, cinnamon variation (page 191)

Pastel sprinkles, for decorating

Edible glitter, for decorating (I use CK)

1. Preheat the oven to 350°F (180°C) and position the racks in the centre of the oven. Line two cupcake pans with 24 cupcake liners.

2. Make the Glorious Gingerbread Cake batter (steps 2 and 3). Divide the batter evenly among the liners and bake for 19 to 22 minutes, until a toothpick inserted in the middle of the cupcakes comes out clean. Allow the cupcakes to cool in the pans for about 5 minutes before removing them from the pans and placing them on a wire rack to cool completely.

3. Make the Cinnamon Cream Cheese Frosting. Fit a pastry bag with a large piping tip and half fill with the frosting. Pipe swirls on each cupcake, beginning in the middle and swirling up and out. Top with sprinkles and glitter.

4. Cupcakes will keep in a container, covered loosely with plastic wrap, at room temperature, for up to 2 days.

Cookies and Cream Cupcakes

This cupcake was made for the Oreo lover! In the past, I've made a more chocolate-focused version of this cupcake, but this recipe is a little lighter and still packed with cookie goodness. Drizzled with ganache and topped with sprinkles, they are simply irresistible.

Makes 12 cupcakes

CUPCAKES

About 10 Oreo cookies

2 cups (230 g) cake flour, sifted

¾ cup (150 g) granulated sugar

2½ teaspoons baking powder

½ teaspoon salt

½ cup (115 g) unsalted butter, cut into pieces, room temperature

¾ cup buttermilk, room temperature

1 teaspoon pure vanilla extract

2 large egg whites, room temperature

1 large egg, room temperature

FOR FROSTING AND DECORATING

1 batch Chocolate Ganache (page 196)

1 batch Bake Shop Vanilla Frosting, cookies and cream variation (page 190)

Pastel sprinkles

1. Preheat the oven to 350°F (180°C). Line a cupcake pan with 12 cupcakes liners.

2. Finely crush the Oreo cookies in a resealable plastic bag using a rolling pin or pulse in a food processor. You should have ¾ cup crumbs. Scrape into a small bowl and set aside.

3. In the bowl of a stand mixer fitted with the paddle attachment, stir together the flour, sugar, baking powder and salt. Mix on low speed until blended. With the mixer running on low speed, add the butter, a few pieces at a time, mixing until the mixture is crumbly.

4. In a liquid measuring cup or a small bowl, whisk together the buttermilk and vanilla. With the mixer running on low speed, pour two-thirds of the buttermilk mixture into the bowl with the flour mixture and mix until the batter comes together. Turn the mixer up to medium speed and beat for about 90 seconds, until the batter has doubled in volume. Stop the mixer and scrape down the sides and bottom of the bowl with a rubber spatula.

5. Add the egg whites and egg to the remaining buttermilk mixture and whisk together with a fork. Pour half of the mixture into the mixer bowl and beat on medium speed to combine, about 15 seconds. Stop the mixer, add the remaining egg mixture and beat for an additional 15 seconds on medium speed. Fold in the crushed Oreos with a rubber spatula.

6. Divide the batter evenly among the liners and bake for 18 to 22 minutes, until a toothpick inserted in the centre of the cupcakes comes out clean. Immediately remove the cupcakes from the cupcake pan and place on a wire rack to cool completely.

7. While the cupcakes are cooling, make the Chocolate Ganache and leave out on the countertop to cool.

8. Once the cupcakes have cooled completely, make the Cookies and Cream Frosting. Fit a pastry bag with a large piping tip and half fill with the frosting. Pipe swirls onto the cupcakes. Use a spoon to drizzle the ganache over each cupcake, then top with sprinkles.

9. Cupcakes will keep in a container, covered loosely with plastic wrap, at room temperature, for up to 2 days.

Vanilla Cotton Candy Cupcakes

My love of both cotton candy and vanilla was the inspiration behind these cupcakes. The light sweetness of the vanilla cupcake perfectly balances out the sugary-sweet cotton candy frosting. To avoid a sticky mess, be sure to top with cotton candy immediately before serving.

Makes 12 cupcakes

CUPCAKES

2 cups plus 2 tablespoons (245 g) cake flour, sifted

1 cup plus 2 tablespoons (225 g) granulated sugar

2½ teaspoons baking powder

½ teaspoon salt

½ cup (115 g) unsalted butter, cut into pieces, room temperature

¾ cup buttermilk, room temperature

2½ teaspoons pure vanilla extract

2 large egg whites, room temperature

1 large egg, room temperature

FOR FROSTING AND DECORATING

1 batch Bake Shop Vanilla Frosting, cotton candy variation (page 190)

1 to 2 drops pink gel food colouring

1 tub (2 ounces/56 g) cotton candy

1. Preheat the oven to 350°F (180°C). Line a cupcake pan with 12 cupcake liners.

2. In the bowl of a stand mixer fitted with the paddle attachment, combine the flour, sugar, baking powder and salt. Mix on low speed until blended. With the mixer running on low speed, add the butter, a few pieces at a time, mixing until the mixture is crumbly.

3. In a liquid measuring cup or small bowl, whisk together the buttermilk and vanilla. With the mixer running on low speed, pour two-thirds of the buttermilk mixture into the bowl with the flour mixture and mix until the batter comes together. Turn the mixer up to medium speed and beat for about 90 seconds, until the batter has gained volume. Stop the mixer and scrape down the sides and bottom of the bowl with a rubber spatula.

4. Add the egg whites and egg to the remaining buttermilk mixture and whisk together with a fork. Pour half of the mixture into the mixer bowl and mix on low speed until some of the liquid has been incorporated, then beat on medium speed to combine completely, 15 to 20 seconds. Stop the mixer, add the remaining egg mixture and beat for an additional 15 seconds on medium speed.

5. Divide the batter evenly among the liners and bake for 18 to 20 minutes, until a toothpick inserted in the centre of the cupcakes comes out clean. Immediately remove the cupcakes from the cupcake pan and place on a wire rack to cool completely.

6. While the cupcakes are cooling, make the Cotton Candy Frosting, adding a few drops of the pink food colouring with the vanilla. Fit a pastry bag with a large piping tip and half fill with the frosting. Pipe swirls onto the cupcakes. Right before serving, top with a puff of cotton candy.

7. Cupcakes (without cotton candy) will keep in a container, covered loosely with plastic wrap, at room temperature, for up to 2 days.

Red Velvet Cupcakes

These super-moist cupcakes are sure to please even the pickiest of eaters. Topped with my cream cheese frosting and heart-shaped sprinkles, they make the perfect Valentine's Day dessert.

Makes 12 cupcakes

CUPCAKES

1½ cups (175 g) cake flour, sifted

1 cup (200 g) granulated sugar

2 tablespoons Dutch-processed cocoa powder

1 teaspoon baking soda

½ teaspoon baking powder

½ teaspoon salt

½ cup plus 2 tablespoons buttermilk, room temperature

¼ cup vegetable oil

¼ cup sour cream

¼ cup hot water

2 tablespoons red liquid food colouring (no-taste, if possible)

1 large egg, room temperature

1 teaspoon white vinegar

1 teaspoon pure vanilla extract

FOR FROSTING AND DECORATING

1 batch Cream Cheese Frosting (page 191)

Heart-shaped sprinkles

1. Preheat the oven to 325°F (160°C). Line a cupcake pan with 12 cupcake liners.

2. In the bowl of a stand mixer fitted with the paddle attachment, combine the flour, sugar, cocoa powder, baking soda, baking powder and salt. Mix on low speed until blended, about 20 seconds.

3. In a small bowl, combine the buttermilk, vegetable oil, sour cream, hot water, food colouring, egg, vinegar and vanilla. Pour into the bowl with the dry ingredients and mix on low speed until just combined. Turn the mixer up to medium speed and beat for 30 seconds. Stop the mixer and scrape down the sides and bottom of the bowl with a rubber spatula, then beat again on medium speed for an additional 30 seconds.

4. Divide the batter evenly among the liners and bake for 20 to 23 minutes, until a toothpick inserted in the centre of the cupcakes comes out clean. Allow the cupcakes to cool for about 5 minutes before removing them from the pan and placing them on a wire rack to cool completely.

5. Make the Cream Cheese Frosting. Fit a pastry bag with a large piping tip and half fill with the frosting. Pipe swirls onto the cupcakes. Finish with sprinkles.

6. Cupcakes will keep in a container, covered loosely with plastic wrap, at room temperature, for up to 2 days.

Cherry Almond Fairy Cakes

These little cupcakes make the most adorable treats to serve at an afternoon tea or a baby shower. For a pop of bright colour, top them with sprinkles or crushed candy of your choice.

Makes 20 fairy cakes

CUPCAKES

2 cups plus 2 tablespoons (245 g) cake flour, sifted

1 cup (200 g) granulated sugar

2½ teaspoons baking powder

½ teaspoon salt

½ cup (115 g) unsalted butter, cut into pieces, room temperature

½ cup plus 2 tablespoons buttermilk, room temperature

2 tablespoons maraschino cherry juice

½ teaspoon pure almond extract

½ teaspoon pure vanilla extract

2 large egg whites, room temperature

1 large egg, room temperature

¼ cup diced maraschino cherries

FOR ICING AND DECORATING

1 batch Sweet Sugar Glaze (page 196)

20 maraschino cherries

1. Preheat the oven to 350°F (180°C) and position the racks in the centre of the oven. Line two cupcake pans with 20 cupcake liners.

2. In the bowl of a stand mixer fitted with the paddle attachment, combine the flour, sugar, baking powder and salt. Mix on low speed until blended. With the mixer running on low speed, add the butter, a few pieces at a time, mixing until the mixture is crumbly.

3. In a liquid measuring cup or small bowl, whisk together the buttermilk, cherry juice and almond and vanilla extracts. With the mixer running on low speed, pour about two-thirds of the buttermilk mixture into the bowl with the flour mixture and mix until the batter comes together. Turn the mixer up to medium speed and beat for about 90 seconds, until the batter has gained volume. Stop the mixer and scrape down the sides and bottom of the bowl with a rubber spatula.

4. Add the egg whites and egg to the remaining buttermilk mixture and whisk together with a fork to combine. Pour half of the mixture into the mixer bowl and mix on low speed until some of the liquid has been incorporated, then beat on medium speed to combine completely, about 15 to 20 seconds. Stop the mixer, add the remaining egg mixture and beat for an additional 15 seconds on medium speed. Fold in the diced cherries with a rubber spatula.

5. Divide the batter evenly among the liners and bake for 16 to 20 minutes, until a toothpick inserted in the centre of the cupcakes comes out clean. Immediately remove the cupcakes from the cupcake pans and place on a wire rack to cool completely.

6. Once the cupcakes have cooled, make the glaze. Spoon about 1 tablespoon of the glaze over each little cake, allowing it to settle into a nice, even coating. Place a cherry on top of each one.

7. Cupcakes will keep in a container, covered loosely with plastic wrap, at room temperature, for up to 2 days.

Gourmet Cookies

Vanilla Bean Shortbread

These melt-in-your-mouth cookies are a favourite with my friends year-round. They're not overly sweet, which makes them the perfect treat for those without a big sweet tooth. Keep them simple with vanilla bean paste, or try one of the flavour variations for a fun twist.

Makes 24 medium cookies

2 cups (450 g) unsalted butter, room temperature

1 cup (125 g) confectioners' sugar

1 tablespoon vanilla bean paste
(or 2 teaspoons pure vanilla extract)

4½ cups (565 g) all-purpose flour

Flavour Variations

Earl Grey: Add 2 tablespoons finely ground Earl Grey tea leaves in place of the vanilla bean paste.

Lavender and Lemon: Add 1 tablespoon finely ground food-grade lavender flowers and 2 tablespoons finely grated lemon zest in place of the vanilla bean paste.

Sweet Tip

You'll probably notice that most of my cookie recipes don't require you to transfer them to a wire rack to cool after baking. The cookies are purposely under-baked ever-so-slightly, so that once they're removed from the oven, they'll finish baking thanks to the heat from the baking sheets.

1. Preheat the oven to 350°F (180°C) and position the racks in the centre of the oven. Line two baking sheets with parchment paper.

2. In the bowl of a stand mixer fitted with the paddle attachment, beat the butter on medium speed until creamy, about 15 seconds. Add the sugar and mix on low speed to incorporate, then add the vanilla bean paste. Beat on medium speed until well mixed, about 10 seconds.

3. With the mixer running on low speed, gradually add the flour. Once the dough comes together, stop the mixer and scrape down the sides of the bowl to release any clinging flour. Mix again on low speed just until the dough is well mixed.

4. Divide the dough into two balls and place each one on a sheet of parchment paper. Pat with the palm of your hand to flatten slightly, then place another sheet of parchment paper on top. Place two ¼-inch rolling sticks on either side of the parchment paper and then use a rolling pin to roll out the dough to an even thickness. Repeat with the other ball of dough.

5. Use a cookie cutter to cut out cookies and place them on the prepared baking sheets, spacing them about an inch apart (they won't spread much at all). Bake for 15 to 18 minutes, until the cookies are just firm. Allow the cookies to cool completely on the baking sheets.

6. Cookies will keep in an airtight container for up to 2 weeks.

Confetti Sprinkle Cookies

Buttery, slightly chewy and dotted with confetti sprinkles, these cookies are one of my best-loved sweets. Serve them warm with a glass of milk, or for a frosty twist, sandwich a scoop of Easy Macaron Ice Cream (page 147) between two cookies.

Makes 18 medium cookies

2½ cups (315 g) all-purpose flour

1¼ cups plus 2 tablespoons (160 g) cake flour, sifted

1 teaspoon baking powder

½ teaspoon salt

¾ cup (170 g) unsalted butter, room temperature

1¾ cups (350 g) granulated sugar

2 large eggs, room temperature

2 teaspoons pure vanilla extract

½ cup confetti sprinkles

Sweet Tip

Trying to decide which sprinkles to use? I've found that jimmies and confetti sequins work best, so I often use a fifty-fifty blend of each.

1. Preheat the oven to 350°F (180°C) and position the racks in the centre of the oven. Line three baking sheets with parchment paper.

2. In a medium bowl, whisk together the all-purpose and cake flours, baking powder and salt.

3. In the bowl of a stand mixer fitted with the paddle attachment, beat the butter and sugar until light and fluffy, about 2 minutes. Add the eggs, one at a time, then add the vanilla and beat to combine. Stop the mixer and scrape down the sides of the bowl with a rubber spatula.

4. Add the flour mixture all at once and mix on low speed until the dough comes together. Stop the mixer and scrape down the sides and bottom of the bowl again. Add the sprinkles and mix on low speed until incorporated.

5. Scoop out the cookie dough ¼ cup at a time, roll into balls and place on the prepared baking sheets, placing no more than 6 cookies on each sheet. Flatten slightly with the palm of your hand.

6. Bake for 12 to 14 minutes, until the cookies are just set around the edges, trying your best not to let the cookies brown. Allow the cookies to cool on the baking sheets for about 10 minutes before moving them to a wire rack to cool completely.

7. Cookies will keep in an airtight container for up to 5 days.

Giant Gingerbread Cuties

Gingerbread cookies hold a special place in my heart, as they were some of the first cookies that I ever learned to bake. Standing on a stepstool at the kitchen counter, I would help my mom cut out shapes and then wait impatiently as the cookies baked in the oven. I only make these during the holidays, but each time I do, I'm flooded with fond memories of my childhood.

Makes about six 8-inch cookies

COOKIES

5 cups (625 g) all-purpose flour

1 tablespoon baking powder

1 teaspoon baking soda

¼ teaspoon salt

2 tablespoons ground ginger

1 tablespoon cinnamon

¼ teaspoon nutmeg

½ cup (115 g) unsalted butter, room temperature

1½ cups (330 g) packed brown sugar

2 large eggs, room temperature

1 cup molasses

2 teaspoons pure vanilla extract

FOR ICING AND DECORATING

1 batch Royal Icing (page 194)

3 to 5 drops black gel food colouring

Pink heart sprinkles, for cheeks

Doughnut or round sprinkles, for buttons

1. In a medium bowl, whisk together the flour, baking powder, baking soda, salt, ginger, cinnamon and nutmeg.

2. In the bowl of a stand mixer fitted with the paddle attachment, beat the butter and brown sugar until blended. Add the eggs, one at a time, beating until combined, then add the molasses and vanilla and mix until well blended. Stop the mixer and scrape down the sides of the bowl with a rubber spatula, then mix on low speed to blend.

3. With the mixer running on low speed, gradually add the flour mixture. Once the dough comes together, stop the mixer and scrape down the sides of the bowl to release any clinging flour. Mix again on low speed until just combined.

4. Remove the dough from the bowl and divide it into two balls. Place one ball between two sheets of parchment paper and roll out to an even ¼-inch thickness. Repeat with the other ball of dough. Keeping them between the parchment, slide both rolled-out doughs onto the back of a baking sheet and refrigerate until firm, about 30 minutes.

5. Meanwhile, preheat the oven to 350°F (180°C) and position the racks in the centre of the oven. Line three baking sheets with parchment paper.

6. Remove one sheet of dough from the refrigerator, peel off the top piece of parchment and use an 8-inch cookie cutter to cut out 2 gingerbread men. Repeat with the second sheet of dough. Gather up the remaining scraps of dough and repeat for the final two cookies. Place the cookies on the prepared baking sheets, spacing them about 2 inches apart, and pop into the freezer until firm, at least 25 minutes.

7. Bake the cookies for 15 to 18 minutes, until just golden brown at the edges. Allow the cookies to cool completely on the baking sheets.

8. Once the cookies have cooled, make the royal icing. Fit a small pastry bag with a small plain piping tip (I use a Wilton #3 tip), spoon some of the royal icing into the bag and secure with a binder clip. Pipe a border around the perimeter of each of the gingerbread cuties.

9. Add the black food colouring to the remaining royal icing and stir to blend. Fit a small pastry bag with a small piping tip (I use a Wilton #2 tip), spoon the black royal icing into the bag and secure with a binder clip. Pipe eyes and a smile onto the cookies. Apply a small amount of icing to the backs of the sprinkles for the cheeks and buttons and gently press them onto the cookies until they stick. Allow the cookies to dry for at least 4 hours before storing or packaging.

10. Cookies will keep in an airtight container or in sealed cellophane bags for up to 2 weeks.

Classic Chocolate Chip Cookies

Crunchy around the edges and chewy in the middle—that's how these cookies bake up. For a fun flavour twist, feel free to swap out half of the semi-sweet chocolate chips for white chocolate chips.

Makes 18 large cookies

1¾ cups (220 g) all-purpose flour

1¼ cups (160 g) bread flour

1 teaspoon baking soda

½ teaspoon salt

1 cup (225 g) unsalted butter, room temperature

1 cup (220 g) packed brown sugar

¾ cup (150 g) granulated sugar

2 large eggs, room temperature

1 teaspoon pure vanilla extract

1½ cups (265 g) semi-sweet chocolate chips

1. Preheat the oven to 350°F (180°C) and position the racks in the centre of the oven. Line three baking sheets with parchment paper.

2. In a small bowl, whisk together the all-purpose and bread flours, baking soda and salt.

3. In the bowl of a stand mixer fitted with the paddle attachment, beat the butter for about 30 seconds, until smooth and creamy. Add the brown and granulated sugars and beat on medium speed until light and fluffy, about 2 minutes. Add the eggs, one at a time, then add the vanilla and beat to combine. Stop the mixer and scrape down the sides and bottom of the bowl with a rubber spatula, then mix on low speed to combine.

4. Add the flour mixture all at once and mix on low speed until the dough comes together. Stop the mixer and scrape down the sides and bottom of the bowl again. Add the chocolate chips and mix on low speed until incorporated.

5. Scoop out the cookie dough ¼ cup at a time, roll into balls and place on the prepared baking sheets, placing no more than 6 cookies on each sheet. Flatten slightly with the palm of your hand.

6. Bake for 10 to 13 minutes, until the cookies are just set and are slightly browned around the edges. Allow the cookies to cool completely on the baking sheets.

7. Cookies will keep in an airtight container for up to 5 days.

Double Chocolate Cookies

These cookies were made for serious chocolate cravings. They're delicious on their own, but are also yummy when filled with Eggless Chocolate Chip Cookie Dough (page 197). For a minty twist, use mint chocolate chips in place of the semi-sweet chocolate chips.

Makes 18 large cookies

1½ cups (190 g) all-purpose flour

1¼ cups (160 g) bread flour

½ cup (55 g) Dutch-processed cocoa powder

1 teaspoon baking soda

¼ teaspoon kosher salt

1 cup (225 g) unsalted butter, room temperature

1 cup (220 g) packed brown sugar

¾ cup (150 g) granulated sugar

2 large eggs, room temperature

1 teaspoon pure vanilla extract

1½ cups (265 g) semi-sweet chocolate chips

Sweet Tip

Be sure not to over-bake the cookies. They will continue to bake and firm up after they're removed from the oven, and you'll end up with delightfully soft chocolate perfection.

1. Preheat the oven to 350°F (180°C) and position the racks in the centre of the oven. Line three baking sheets with parchment paper.

2. In a medium bowl, whisk together the all-purpose and bread flours, cocoa powder, baking soda and salt.

3. In the bowl of a stand mixer fitted with the paddle attachment, beat the butter for about 30 seconds, until smooth and creamy. Add the brown and granulated sugars and beat on medium speed until light and fluffy, about 2 minutes. Add the eggs, one at a time, beating well after each addition. Finally, add the vanilla and mix until well blended. Stop the mixer and scrape down the sides of the bowl with a rubber spatula.

4. Add the flour mixture all at once and mix on low speed to incorporate. Stop the mixer and scrape down the sides and bottom of the bowl again, then mix on low speed until blended. Add the chocolate chips and mix on low speed until incorporated.

5. Scoop out the cookie dough ¼ cup at a time, roll into balls and place on the prepared baking sheets, placing no more than 6 cookies on each sheet. Flatten slightly with the palm of your hand.

6. Bake for 15 to 18 minutes, until the cookies are just set around the edges and still a little soft in the middle. Allow the cookies to cool completely on the baking sheets.

7. Cookies will keep in an airtight container for up to 5 days.

Cookie Dough Sandwich Cookies

Without a doubt, these cookies are the ones I'm most often asked to bring to parties. Some of my friends pop them into the freezer, taking them out to thaw when they have a craving or even simply eating them as a frozen treat. Whether you serve them right away or store them in the freezer for later is up to you, but either way, they'll be very much enjoyed.

Makes 36 cookies; 18 medium sandwiches

1 batch Classic Chocolate Chip Cookies dough (page 97)

1 batch Eggless Chocolate Chip Cookie Dough (page 197)

Sweet Tip

Craving a frozen treat? Pop the sandwiches in the freezer for 1 to 2 hours and you'll have some lovely Frozen Cookie Dough Sandwiches.

1. Preheat the oven to 350°F (180°C). Line three baking sheets with parchment paper.

2. Make the Classic Chocolate Chip Cookies dough (steps 2 through 4). Scoop out the cookie dough 2 tablespoons at a time, roll into balls and place on the prepared baking sheets, placing 12 cookies on each sheet and spacing them at least 2 inches apart. Flatten slightly with the palm of your hand.

3. Bake for 9 to 12 minutes, until the cookies are just set and are slightly brown around the edges. Allow the cookies to cool completely on the baking sheets.

4. While the cookies are cooling, make the Eggless Chocolate Chip Cookie Dough. Fit a pastry bag with a large round piping tip and half fill with the cookie dough.

5. Turn half of the cooled cookies upside down and pipe a dollop of the filling onto the bottom, right in the middle of each cookie. Place the remaining cookies, right side up, on top of the filling and press down gently, sandwiching the filling between the two cookies.

6. Cookies will keep in an airtight container in the refrigerator for up to 2 days. Allow the cookies to stand at room temperature for 1 to 2 hours before serving.

Walter's Peanut Butter Sandwich Cookies

Walter and I met on Valentine's Day. The following week, he returned to my shop with a friend and sat down to drink his coffee and eat his peanut butter sandwich cookie. This became a pleasant routine. Several days a week he would drop by and order the same thing, always joking with us and talking to the customers in line behind him, being sure to tell them that the peanut butter sandwich cookie was the thing to order. This schedule of jokes and cookies continued until the day I closed my shop doors, and although I no longer see Walter, I think of him fondly every time I make these cookies.

Makes 12 cookies; 6 large sandwiches

SANDWICH COOKIES

1¾ cups (220 g) all-purpose flour

¾ cup (90 g) bread flour

1 teaspoon baking soda

½ teaspoon salt

¾ cup (170 g) unsalted butter, room temperature

¾ cup (180 g) smooth peanut butter

¾ cup (165 g) packed brown sugar

½ cup (100 g) granulated sugar

1 large egg, room temperature

1 teaspoon pure vanilla extract

PEANUT BUTTER CREAM FILLING

¾ cup (180 g) smooth peanut butter

6 tablespoons (85 g) unsalted butter, room temperature

2 cups (250 g) confectioners' sugar

⅓ cup heavy (35%) cream, room temperature

1 teaspoon pure vanilla extract

1. Preheat the oven to 350°F (180°C) and position the racks in the centre of the oven. Line two baking sheets with parchment paper.

2. In a medium bowl, whisk together the all-purpose and bread flours, baking soda and salt.

3. In the bowl of a stand mixer fitted with the paddle attachment, combine the butter and peanut butter. Beat together on medium speed until creamy, about 15 seconds. Add the brown and granulated sugars and beat on medium speed for 2 minutes. Stop the mixer and scrape down the sides and bottom of the bowl with a rubber spatula. Add the egg and vanilla, then beat on medium speed until just combined.

4. Add the flour mixture all at once and mix on low speed until the dough comes together. Stop the mixer and scrape down the sides and bottom of the bowl again, then mix on low speed just until combined.

5. Scoop out the cookie dough ¼ cup at a time, roll into balls and place on the baking sheets, placing no more than 6 cookies on each sheet and spacing them 2 to 3 inches apart. Flatten slightly with the palm of your hand.

6. Bake for 14 to 17 minutes, until cracks form and the cookies are golden brown. Allow the cookies to cool completely on the baking sheets.

7. Once the cookies have cooled, make the Peanut Butter Cream Filling. Place the peanut butter and the butter in the bowl of a stand mixer fitted with the paddle attachment. Beat on medium speed until smooth and creamy, about 15 seconds. Stop the mixer and add the confectioners' sugar, cream and vanilla, then mix together on low speed until combined. Turn the mixer up to medium speed and beat until light and fluffy, about 1 minute. Stop the mixer and scrape down the sides and bottom of the bowl with a rubber spatula, then beat again on medium speed for 10 seconds.

8. Turn half of the cookies upside down and use a spoon to spread the filling onto each one. Place the remaining cookies, right side up, on top of the filling and press down lightly to help them stick to the filling.

9. Unfilled cookies will keep in an airtight container for up to 5 days. Filled cookies will keep in an airtight container in the refrigerator for up to 2 days, or in the freezer for up to 1 month.

Brown Butter S'more Sandwich Cookies

This is, hands down, one of my favourite recipes. The buttery cookies are delicious on their own, but when sandwiched together with chocolate ganache and toasty marshmallow, they transform into something decadent and, well, addictive. Be sure to have plenty of napkins on hand, as these tend to get a little messy.

Makes 16 medium cookies; 8 medium sandwiches

SANDWICH COOKIES

¾ cup (170 g) unsalted butter

½ cup (110 g) packed brown sugar

¼ cup plus 2 tablespoons (75 g) granulated sugar

1 large egg, room temperature

1 teaspoon pure vanilla extract

¾ cup plus 2 tablespoons (110 g) all-purpose flour

½ cup plus 2 tablespoons (80 g) bread flour

½ teaspoon baking soda

½ teaspoon salt

FOR FILLING AND FROSTING

1 batch Chocolate Ganache (page 196)

1 batch Dreamy Marshmallow Frosting (page 192)

1. Place a heatproof bowl on a wire rack and set aside.

2. Place the butter in a medium saucepan. Melt over medium-low heat, stirring often with a wooden spoon, until the butter is browned. Be sure to keep an eye on the butter, as it can quickly go from perfectly browned to burnt. Pour the butter into the heatproof bowl, making sure to include the brown bits from the bottom of the pan. Set aside until cooled. Transfer to the refrigerator and chill, stirring often with a rubber spatula until the butter is creamy and spreadable, about 45 minutes.

3. Preheat the oven to 350°F (180°C) and position the racks in the centre of the oven. Line two baking sheets with parchment paper.

4. Scrape the browned butter into the bowl of a stand mixer fitted with the paddle attachment. Add the brown and granulated sugars and beat on medium speed until light and fluffy, about 2 minutes. Stop the mixer and scrape down the sides of the bowl with a rubber spatula. Add the egg and the vanilla, then beat on medium speed until blended, about 15 seconds.

5. In a small bowl, whisk together the all-purpose and bread flours, baking soda and salt. Add to the mixer bowl all at once and mix on low speed to incorporate.

6. Scoop out the cookie dough 2 tablespoons at a time, roll into balls and place on the prepared baking sheets, placing 8 cookies on each sheet and spacing them at least 2 inches apart. Flatten slightly with the palm of your hand.

7. Bake for 10 to 13 minutes, until the edges of the cookies begin to brown. Allow the cookies to cool completely on the baking sheets.

8. When ready to serve, make the Chocolate Ganache and set aside to cool.

9. Make the Dreamy Marshmallow Frosting. Fit a pastry bag with a large piping tip and half fill with the frosting. Turn half of the cookies upside down and pipe a border around the perimeter of each one, creating a little well. Spoon a little of the Chocolate Ganache into the centres. Place the remaining cookies, right side up, on top of the filling and press down very gently.

10. Place the sandwiches on a baking sheet. Use a kitchen torch to carefully brown the edges of the marshmallow frosting, turning the sandwiches as you go to prevent scorching. Serve immediately.

11. Unfilled cookies will keep in an airtight container for up to 5 days.

Lemon Delight Cookies

My friend Sarah and I frequent a local diner that used to serve the best lemon cookies either of us had ever eaten. Then one day, the cookies disappeared from the menu, leaving us heartbroken—and with major cravings. So I set to work in the kitchen, determined to bake something that came close to those delightful little cookies that we both loved so much, and this recipe was the result.

Makes about 18 medium cookies

COOKIES

2½ cups (315 g) all-purpose flour

1¼ cups (145 g) cake flour, sifted

1¼ teaspoons baking powder

¼ teaspoon salt

¾ cup (170 g) unsalted butter, room temperature

1¾ cups (350 g) granulated sugar

2 large eggs, room temperature

2½ teaspoons pure vanilla extract

2½ teaspoons lemon extract

3 tablespoons lemon zest

FOR ICING

1 batch Sweet Sugar Glaze, lemon variation (page 196)

1. Preheat the oven to 350°F (180°C) and position the racks in the centre of the oven. Line three baking sheets with parchment paper.

2. In a medium bowl, whisk together the all-purpose and cake flours, baking powder and salt. Set aside.

3. In the bowl of a stand mixer fitted with the paddle attachment, beat the butter and sugar together on medium speed until light and fluffy. Add the eggs, one at a time, beating until blended. Add the vanilla, lemon extract and lemon zest and beat to combine. Stop the mixer and scrape down the sides of the bowl with a rubber spatula, then beat on medium speed until blended, about 15 seconds.

4. Add the flour mixture all at once and mix on low speed until the dough comes together. Stop the mixer and scrape down the sides and bottom of the bowl again, then mix on low speed just until combined.

5. Scoop out the cookie dough ¼ cup at a time, roll into balls and place on the prepared baking sheets, placing no more than 6 cookies on each sheet. Flatten slightly with the palm of your hand.

6. Bake for 12 to 14 minutes, until the cookies are just set around the edges, trying your best not to let the cookies brown. Allow the cookies to cool on the baking sheets for about 10 minutes before moving them to a wire rack to cool completely.

7. Once the cookies have cooled, make the Lemon Glaze. Use a spoon to drizzle it back and forth across each cookie, coating each one as much or as little as you like. Allow the glaze to set for at least 10 minutes before serving.

8. Cookies will keep in an airtight container for up to 5 days.

Sugar Cookies Galore

Decorating Sugar Cookies with Royal Icing

I was taught to ice cakes and cookies using a small cone made out of parchment paper, fitted with a piping tip. Since I have no patience for folding paper cones, I instead use a small plastic pastry bag fitted with a piping tip. I fold up the end of my bag and secure it with a binder clip to prevent any icing from popping out of the top. I don't use a coupler, but if you feel that you'd like to use one, go right ahead—it's all about what you feel most comfortable with. I also flood my cookies with Royal Icing (page 194) using a plastic squeeze bottle instead of the traditional pastry bag, as I find it to be less messy and easier to handle.

Filling a Pastry Bag with Royal Icing

1. Snip the tip off of a small pastry bag and fit it with a small plain piping tip (I usually use a Wilton #2 tip).

2. Use a small spoon to fill the bag halfway with royal icing, then fold the corners in and roll the top of the bag down to close. Secure with a binder clip and you're ready to pipe. Note: If you're not piping right away, be sure to cover the tip with a piece of damp paper towel to prevent the icing from drying out.

Filling a Squeeze Bottle with Royal Icing

1. Remove the lid and place the bottle on a flat surface. Slowly pour flood-consistency royal icing into the bottle.

2. Screw the lid on tight and you're ready to ice.

1. Begin by making soft-peak royal icing (see recipe and instructions on page 194). If you're adding colour to your icing, stir in a few drops of gel food colouring. Fit a small pastry bag with a plain piping tip, fill halfway with the icing and secure with a binder clip.

2. Using your dominant hand, hold the bag comfortably between your thumb, index and middle fingers. Apply pressure at the top of the bag, just below the binder clip. Applying even pressure, squeeze the icing onto the edge of the cookie and pipe an icing border all the way around, until you meet the icing where you began. This border acts as a wall, which keeps the flooding icing from running off your cookie. Be sure that the icing is connected all the way around the cookie with no gaps, or else the flooding icing could run off.

3. Turn the remaining icing into flood consistency (see instructions on page 195). Fill a squeeze bottle with the icing. Hold the bottle over the cookie and squeeze the icing out to cover the whole cookie. Use a toothpick to move the icing right to the edges or to fill in any gaps. Be careful not to over-flood your cookies, as applying too much icing will cause it to run right over the edges. Allow your cookies to dry for at least 12 hours before storing or packaging.

Vanilla Sugar Cookies

These buttery, vanilla-flecked cookies continue to be one of the most popular sweets that I've ever baked. We often had trouble keeping them in stock at my shop, and every holiday, they seem to be the most sought-after treat in my kitchen. Decorated or not, these sugar cookies are delicious and a great staple recipe to add to your collection.

Makes 25 medium cookies

4½ cups (565 g) all-purpose flour

½ teaspoon salt

1½ cups (335 g) unsalted butter, room temperature

1½ cups (300 g) granulated sugar

1 large egg, cold

2 teaspoons pure vanilla extract (or 1 tablespoon vanilla bean paste)

1. In a medium bowl, whisk together the flour and salt.

2. In the bowl of a stand mixer fitted with the paddle attachment, beat together the butter and sugar on medium speed until well blended, about 1 minute. (Don't over-mix or your cookies won't hold their shape when baked.) Stop the mixer and scrape down the sides of the bowl with a rubber spatula. Add the egg and the vanilla and beat on medium speed just until combined.

3. With the mixer running on low speed, add the flour mixture all at once and mix until just combined. Stop the mixer and scrape down the sides and bottom of the bowl, then mix again on low speed until the dry ingredients are blended in. Try not to over-mix the dough.

4. Divide the dough into two balls and place each one on a sheet of parchment paper. Pat with the palm of your hand to flatten slightly, then place another sheet of parchment paper on top (SEE PHOTO 1, page 113). Place two ¼-inch rolling sticks on either side of the parchment paper and then use a rolling pin to roll out the dough to an even thickness (SEE PHOTO 2, page 113). Repeat with the other ball of dough. Keeping them between the parchment, slide both rolled doughs onto the back of a baking sheet and pop in the refrigerator until firm, about 25 minutes.

5. Meanwhile, preheat the oven to 350°F (180°C) and position the racks in the centre of the oven. Line three baking sheets with parchment paper.

6. Remove one sheet of dough from the refrigerator, peel off the top piece of parchment paper and use a medium cookie cutter to cut out desired shapes (SEE PHOTO 3, opposite). Repeat with the second sheet of dough. Place the cookies on the prepared baking sheets, spacing them about 2 inches apart, and pop into the freezer until firm, at least 25 minutes. Gather up the remaining dough and repeat.

7. Bake the cookies for 15 to 18 minutes, until just golden brown at the edges. Allow the cookies to cool completely on the baking sheets. Handling warm cookies can cause them to crack or break.

8. Cookies will keep in an airtight container for up to 3 weeks.

Chocolate Sugar Cookies

Dark and buttery, these sugar cookies are easily one of my favourite treats. I prefer to serve them naked (without icing) and let the rich chocolate flavour really take centre stage. However, if it's an iced cookie you're after, whip up a batch of Royal Icing (page 194) and decorate away.

Makes 25 medium cookies

3¾ cups (470 g) all-purpose flour

¾ cup (85 g) Dutch-processed cocoa powder

½ teaspoon salt

1½ cups (335 g) unsalted butter, room temperature

1½ cups (300 g) granulated sugar

1 large egg, cold

1 tablespoon pure vanilla extract

1. In a medium bowl, whisk together the flour, cocoa powder and salt.

2. In the bowl of a stand mixer fitted with the paddle attachment, beat together the butter and sugar on medium speed until well blended, about 1 minute. (Don't over-mix or your cookies won't hold their shape when baked.) Stop the mixer and scrape down the sides of the bowl with a rubber spatula. Add the egg and the vanilla and beat on medium speed just until combined.

3. With the mixer running on low speed, add the flour mixture all at once and mix until just combined. Stop the mixer and scrape down the sides and bottom of the bowl, then mix again on low speed until the dry ingredients are blended in. Try not to over-mix the dough.

4. Divide the dough into two balls and place each one on a sheet of parchment paper. Pat with the palm of your hand to flatten slightly, then place another sheet of parchment paper on top. Place two ¼-inch rolling sticks on either side of the parchment paper and then use a rolling pin to roll out the dough to an even thickness. Repeat with the other ball of dough. Keeping them between the parchment, slide both rolled doughs onto the back of a baking sheet and pop in the refrigerator until firm, about 25 minutes.

5. Meanwhile, preheat the oven to 350°F (180°C) and position the racks in the centre of the oven. Line three baking sheets with parchment paper.

6. Remove one sheet of dough from the refrigerator, peel off the top piece of parchment paper and use a medium cookie cutter to cut out desired shapes. Repeat with the second sheet of dough. Place the cookies on the prepared baking sheets, spacing them about 2 inches apart, and pop into the freezer until firm, at least 25 minutes. Gather up the remaining dough and repeat.

7. Bake the cookies for 15 to 18 minutes, until the edges have set. Allow the cookies to cool completely on the baking sheets. Handling warm cookies can cause them to crack or break.

8. Cookies will keep in an airtight container for up to 3 weeks.

Pretty Pastel Pony Cookies

When I was a little girl, I used to live for the carnival. Each summer, we would pile into the car and drive one hour to the next-biggest town, where my dad would purchase a small roll of tickets and take me to ride the girliest carousel we could find. Inspired by the pastel hues of that beloved carnival ride, these ponies are sure to please both children and children-at-heart alike.

Makes 25 medium cookies

1 batch Vanilla Sugar Cookies dough (page 113)

2 batches Royal Icing (page 194)

1 to 2 drops pink gel food colouring

1 to 2 drops purple gel food colouring

Edible glitter (I use CK) (optional)

Black edible marker (I use Wilton)

Gold lustre dust (I use CK)

1 teaspoon clear alcohol (such as gin or vodka) or lemon extract

1. Line three baking sheets with parchment paper.

2. Make and roll out the Vanilla Sugar Cookies dough (steps 1 through 6), using a medium pony head or horse head cookie cutter to cut out the dough. Place the cookies on the prepared baking sheets, spacing them about 2 inches apart, and pop them into the freezer until firm, at least 25 minutes. Gather up the remaining dough and repeat.

3. While the cookies are firming up, preheat the oven to 350°F (180°C) and position the racks in the centre of the oven.

4. Bake the cookies for 15 to 18 minutes, until just golden brown at the edges. Allow the cookies to cool completely on the baking sheets. Handling warm cookies can cause them to crack or break.

5. Make the royal icing and turn it into soft-peak consistency (see recipe and instructions on page 194). Place about 1½ cups in a medium bowl, cover with a damp tea towel and set aside for later.

6. Fit a small pastry bag with a small piping tip (I use a Wilton #2 tip), half fill with the royal icing and close with a binder clip. Pipe a border of icing all the way around each cookie, making sure there are no gaps in your border.

7. Once all the cookies have a border, turn the royal icing into flood consistency (see instructions on page 195) and fill a squeeze bottle with the icing. Keep the remaining icing covered with a damp tea towel. Carefully flood each cookie. Allow them to dry for at least 5 hours.

8. Divide the reserved soft-peak icing between 2 bowls. Use the food colouring to tint one bowl purple and one pink. Fit a small pastry bag with a small plain piping tip (I use a Wilton #2 tip) and fill with some of the purple icing. Cover the tip with a piece of damp paper towel to prevent the icing from drying out, and set aside. Fit a larger pastry bag with a small open star tip (I use a Wilton #17 tip). Spoon in the pink icing, smearing it along one side of the bag, then spoon in the remaining purple icing, smearing it along the opposite side. Don't worry about the two colours of icing blending together. When the pastry bag is about half-full, roll down the top and secure with a binder clip. Pipe the mane of the pony, beginning at the bottom of the mane and working your way up. Sprinkle a pinch of edible glitter over the mane, if desired. Repeat with the remaining cookies.

9. Use the small bag of purple icing to pipe the noseband, cheek piece and headpiece on the pony, adding two extra dots of icing for the metal pieces. Use the edible marker to draw on eyelashes. Allow the cookies to dry completely, at least 5 hours.

10. Once the cookies have dried, mix the lustre dust and clear alcohol together with a small food-only paintbrush to make a paint. Brush the two dots of icing with a small amount of the paint, then allow to dry for at least 1 hour before storing or packaging.

11. Dried cookies will keep in an airtight container or in sealed cellophane bags for up to 3 weeks.

Lunchbox Love Note Cookies

When I was three or four years old, I decided that I wanted to start packing my dad's lunchbox for him. He's always had a sweet tooth (and a not-so-secret stash of cookies tucked away somewhere), so I figured I would put together the ultimate sandwich for him: butter and granulated sugar on bread. I would include a handwritten note in his lunchbox as well. These little note cookies are sweet surprises that are just as simple to make.

Makes 25 medium cookies

1 batch Vanilla Sugar Cookies dough (page 113)

2 batches Royal Icing (page 194)

Blue, black, pink and red edible markers (I use Wilton)

1. Line three baking sheets with parchment paper.

2. Make and roll out the Vanilla Sugar Cookies dough (steps 1 through 6), using a medium rectangle cookie cutter to cut out the dough. Place the cookies on the prepared baking sheets, spacing them about 2 inches apart, and pop them into the freezer until firm, at least 25 minutes. Gather up the remaining dough and repeat.

3. While the cookies are firming up, preheat the oven to 350°F (180°C) and position the racks in the centre of the oven.

4. Bake the cookies for 15 to 18 minutes, until just golden brown at the edges. Allow the cookies to cool completely on the baking sheets. Handling warm cookies can cause them to crack or break.

5. Make the royal icing and turn it into soft-peak consistency (see recipe and instructions on page 194). Fit a small pastry bag with a small plain piping tip (I use a Wilton #2 tip), half fill with the royal icing and close with a binder clip. Pipe a border of icing all the way around each cookie, making sure there are no gaps in your border.

6. Once all the cookies have a border, turn the royal icing into flood consistency (see instructions on page 195) and fill a squeeze bottle with the icing. Keep the remaining icing covered with a damp tea towel. Carefully flood each cookie. Allow them to dry for at least 8 hours or overnight.

7. Once the icing is completely dry, use a ruler and an edible marker to draw straight lines on each cookie. Use different marker colours to write notes for family and friends.

8. Dried cookies will keep in an airtight container or in sealed cellophane bags for up to 3 weeks.

Sprinkly Fairy Wand Cookies

These sprinkle-covered pastel cookies are sure to please the fanciest of little princesses. They're easy to make (kids can help!) and make perfect take-home party treats.

Makes 25 medium cookies

1 batch Vanilla Sugar Cookies dough (page 113)

2 batches Royal Icing (page 194)

1 teaspoon bubblegum flavouring
(I use LorAnn Oils) (optional)

1 drop pink gel food colouring

1 drop turquoise gel food colouring

1 cup pastel sprinkles

Edible gold flakes (I use Cote D'Azur)

1. Line three baking sheets with parchment paper.

2. Make and roll out the Vanilla Sugar Cookies dough (steps 1 through 6), using a medium star cookie cutter to cut out the dough. Place the cookies on the prepared baking sheets, placing about 8 cookies on each sheet and spacing them about 2 inches apart. Insert a lollipop stick into the bottom of each cookie by gently wiggling it back and forth until it is halfway into the dough, being careful not to poke the stick through the front or the back of the cookie. (If it does, gently press a small piece of dough onto the exposed stick and pat to even out.) Pop the cookies into the freezer until firm, at least 25 minutes. Gather up the remaining dough and repeat.

3. While the cookies are firming up, preheat the oven to 350°F (180°C) and position the racks in the centre of the oven.

4. Bake the cookies for 15 to 18 minutes, until just golden brown at the edges. Allow the cookies to cool completely on the baking sheets. Handling warm cookies can cause them to crack or break.

5. Make the royal icing and turn it into soft-peak consistency (see recipe and instructions on page 194). Stir in the bubblegum flavouring, if using. Divide the icing among three bowls. Tint one bowl pale pink and one pale turquoise. Leave the remaining bowl white.

6. Fit three small pastry bags with small plain piping tips (I use a Wilton #3 tip) and half fill each bag: one with pale turquoise, one with pale pink and one with white. Roll down the tops of the bags and close with binder clips. Pipe a border around the edge of each cookie using the various colours of icing. Fill in each cookie with the same colour of icing as the border by piping it back and forth in a sort of scribbling motion, until the cookie is covered in icing. Immediately top with sprinkles and gold flakes. Allow the cookies to dry for at least 8 hours or overnight.

7. Dried cookies will keep in an airtight container or in sealed cellophane bags for up to 3 weeks.

Starry Sky Cookies

I grew up in a small town, far away from the bright city lights. While I've always been a city girl at heart, I often miss being able to look up at the sky and see the stars. The pastel skies on these cookies play host to sweet, puffy clouds and silver stars made of sugar, which is what I always dreamed they would be like when I was a little girl.

Makes 25 medium cookies

1 batch Vanilla Sugar Cookies dough (page 113)

2 batches Royal Icing (page 194)

1 to 2 drops purple gel food colouring

1 to 2 drops pink gel food colouring

Edible silver stars (I use Wilton)

1 cup (125 g) confectioners' sugar

1. Line three baking sheets with parchment paper.

2. Make and roll out the Vanilla Sugar Cookies dough (steps 1 through 6), using a medium round cookie cutter to cut out the dough. Place the cookies on the prepared baking sheets, spacing them about 2 inches apart, and pop into the freezer until firm, at least 25 minutes. Gather up the remaining dough and repeat.

3. While the cookies are firming up, preheat the oven to 350°F (180°C) and position the racks in the centre of the oven.

4. Bake the cookies for 15 to 18 minutes, until just golden brown at the edges. Allow the cookies to cool completely on the baking sheets. Handling warm cookies can cause them to crack or break.

5. Make the royal icing and turn it into soft-peak consistency (see recipe and instructions on page 194). Place ½ cup of the icing in a separate bowl, cover with a damp tea towel and set aside for later. Tint the remaining icing by mixing in a few drops of both the purple and the pink food colouring, until the desired colour is achieved.

6. Fit a small pastry bag with a small plain piping tip (I use a Wilton #2 tip), half fill with the tinted royal icing and close with a binder clip. Pipe a border of icing all the way around each cookie, making sure there are no gaps in your border.

7. Once all the cookies have a border, turn the royal icing into flood consistency (see instructions on page 195) and fill a squeeze bottle with the icing. Keep the remaining icing covered with a damp tea towel. Carefully flood each cookie, then sprinkle a few of the silver stars over each one. Allow the cookies to dry for at least 6 hours.

8. Once the icing has dried, lay a cloud stencil over a cookie. Holding the stencil in place, use a small offset spatula or the back of a spoon to gently spread a thin layer of the reserved white royal icing over the stencil, covering it evenly. Do not remove the stencil.

9. Place some of the confectioners' sugar in a small sifter. Holding it over the cookie, gently tap out the sugar until the icing is covered. Lift the stencil off the cookie. Lift the cookie and gently tap off the excess sugar. If necessary, use a small dry paintbrush to sweep away any excess. Repeat with the remaining cookies. Allow the cookies to dry for at least 8 hours or overnight.

10. Dried cookies will keep in an airtight container or in sealed cellophane bags for up to 3 weeks.

Polka Dot Bunny Cookies

Since opening day, these bunny cookies were a staple in my bakery. Often I would decorate them with eyelashes or a ribbon around the neck, but here, I've added a puff of cotton candy for extra fun. Be sure to apply the cotton candy right before serving, as moisture in the air will quickly turn it into a sticky mess.

Makes 25 medium cookies

1 batch Vanilla Sugar Cookies dough (page 113)

2 batches Royal Icing (page 194)

1 to 2 drops pink gel food colouring

1 tub (2 ounces/56 g) pink cotton candy

1. Line three baking sheets with parchment paper.

2. Make and roll out the Vanilla Sugar Cookies dough (steps 1 through 6), using a medium bunny cookie cutter to cut out the dough. Place the cookies on the prepared baking sheets, spacing them about 2 inches apart, and pop them into the freezer until firm, at least 25 minutes. Gather up the remaining dough and repeat.

3. While the cookies are firming up, preheat the oven to 350°F (180°C) and position the racks in the centre of the oven.

4. Bake the cookies for 15 to 18 minutes, until just golden brown at the edges. Allow the cookies to cool completely on the baking sheets. Handling warm cookies can cause them to crack or break.

5. Make the royal icing and turn it into soft-peak consistency (see recipe and instructions on page 194). Place 2 tablespoons in a small bowl, cover with a damp tea towel and a dinner plate and set aside.

6. Fit a small pastry bag with a small plain piping tip (I use a Wilton #2 tip), half fill with the royal icing and close with a binder clip. Pipe a border of icing all the way around each cookie, making sure there are no gaps in your border.

7. Once all the cookies have a border, turn the royal icing into flood consistency (see instructions on page 195) and fill a squeeze bottle with the icing. Pour about ½ cup of the remaining icing into a small bowl and stir in a few drops of the pink food colouring. Pour the pink icing into another squeeze bottle. Keep the remaining white icing covered with a damp tea towel. Working with one cookie at a time, carefully flood each cookie with white icing and add pink dots immediately after flooding. Allow the cookies to dry for at least 8 hours or overnight.

8. Right before serving, use the back of a spoon to spread a small amount of the reserved soft-peak royal icing onto the tail of each bunny. Gently press a puff of cotton candy onto the wet icing and serve immediately.

9. Dried cookies (without the cotton candy) will keep in an airtight container or in sealed cellophane bags for up to 3 weeks.

Sprinkly Cloud Cookies

These sprinkle-filled clouds will delight dessert lovers of all ages. They can be filled with any type or colour of sprinkles, making them perfect for gender-reveal parties or take-home favours.

Makes 12 medium cookies

1 batch Vanilla Sugar Cookies dough (page 113)

1 batch Royal Icing (page 194)

1 to 2 drops black gel food colouring

Pink lustre dust (I use CK)

Pastel and snowflake sprinkles

1. Line three baking sheets with parchment paper.

2. Make and roll out the Vanilla Sugar Cookies dough (steps 1 through 6), using a medium cloud cookie cutter to cut 36 clouds from the dough. Use a small round or diamond cookie cutter to cut a hole in the centre of 12 of the cookies. Place the cookies on the prepared baking sheets, spacing them about 2 inches apart, and pop them into the freezer until firm, at least 25 minutes. Gather up the remaining dough and repeat.

3. While the cookies are firming up, preheat the oven to 350°F (180°C) and position the racks in the centre of the oven.

4. Bake the cookies for 15 to 18 minutes, until just golden brown at the edges. Allow the cookies to cool completely on the baking sheets. Handling warm cookies can cause them to crack or break.

5. Make the royal icing and turn it into soft-peak consistency (see recipe and instructions on page 194). Place ¼ cup of the icing in a small bowl, cover with a damp tea towel and a dinner plate and set aside for assembling the cookies. Fit a small pastry bag with a small plain piping tip (I use a Wilton #2 tip), half fill with the royal icing and close with a binder clip. Pipe a border of icing all the way around 12 of the solid cookies, making sure there are no gaps in your border.

6. Once the cookies have a border, turn the royal icing into flood consistency (see instructions on page 195) and fill a squeeze bottle with the icing. Keep the remaining icing covered with a damp tea towel. Carefully flood the 12 cookies. Allow them to dry for at least 8 hours or overnight.

7. Once the cookies have dried, spoon 1 to 2 tablespoons of the reserved soft-peak royal icing into another small bowl and stir in the black food colouring. Fit a small pastry bag with a small plain piping tip (I use a Wilton #1 tip), half fill with the royal icing and close with a binder clip. Pipe two eyes, lashes and a mouth onto each one of the iced cookies. While the eyes and mouth are drying, use a small food-only paintbrush to apply lustre dust to the cheeks.

8. Assemble the cookies: Fit a small pastry bag with a small plain piping tip, spoon in the remaining soft-peak white icing and secure with a binder clip. Pipe a small amount of icing onto the underside of a cookie with a hole in it. Place it, icing side down, on an un-iced solid cookie, pressing firmly to secure the two together. Repeat with remaining un-iced cookies. Pour sprinkles into the holes. Working with one cookie at a time, pipe a small amount of icing onto the top of the cookies with holes, then gently place one of the iced cloud cookies on top. Repeat with the remaining cookies. Set aside to dry, 2 to 3 hours.

9. Dried cookies will keep in an airtight container or in sealed cellophane bags for up to 3 weeks.

Cotton Candy Cookies

My love of cotton candy is serious. If we're ever hanging out at a carnival and I disappear, look for the nearest cotton candy cart and that's where you'll find me. There's something so magical about this sugary treat, especially when it's freshly spun and still warm (oh my goodness). I've often made cotton candy–flavoured desserts for customers, but sticking it directly on top of sugar cookies makes it even better.

Makes 25 medium cookies

1 batch Vanilla Sugar Cookies dough (page 113)

2 batches Royal Icing (page 194)

Silver lustre dust (I use CK)

1 teaspoon clear alcohol (vodka or gin) or lemon extract

1 to 2 drops pink gel food colouring

2 tubs (2 ounces/56 g each) pink-and-blue cotton candy

1. Line three baking sheets with parchment paper.

2. Make the Vanilla Sugar Cookie dough (steps 1 through 6), using a medium ice cream cone cookie cutter to cut out the dough. Place the cookies on the prepared baking sheets, spacing them about 2 inches apart, and pop them into the freezer until firm, at least 25 minutes. Gather up the remaining dough and repeat.

3. While the cookies are firming up, preheat the oven to 350°F (180°C) and position the racks in the centre of the oven.

4. Bake the cookies for 15 to 18 minutes, until just golden brown at the edges. Allow the cookies to cool completely on the baking sheets. Handling warm cookies can cause them to crack or break.

5. Make the royal icing and turn it into soft-peak consistency (see recipe and instructions on page 194). Place about 1½ cups in a small bowl, cover with a damp tea towel and set aside.

6. Fit a small pastry bag with a small plain piping tip (I use a Wilton #2 tip), half fill with the royal icing and close with a binder clip. Pipe a border of icing all the way around each cookie, making sure there are no gaps in your border.

7. Once all the cookies have a border, turn the royal icing into flood consistency (see instructions on page 195) and fill a squeeze bottle with the icing. Keep the remaining icing covered with a damp tea towel. Carefully flood each cookie with white icing. Allow the cookies to dry for at least 8 hours or overnight.

8. Mix a little bit of the silver lustre dust with the clear alcohol. Use a small food-only paintbrush to paint stripes on the "cone" part of each cookie.

9. Right before serving, stir the pink food colouring into the reserved soft-peak royal icing. Use the back of a spoon to spread a small amount of the icing onto the "ice cream" part of the cookie. Gently press a large puff of cotton candy onto the wet, just-applied soft-peak royal icing and serve immediately.

10. Dried cookies (without the cotton candy) will keep in an airtight container or in sealed cellophane bags for up to 3 weeks.

Whimsical Treats

Cookies and Cream Spoons

These 100 percent edible spoons are great on their own, but even better when paired with another treat! Serve them with Mint Chip Cheesecake Cups (page 143) or Easy Macaron Ice Cream (page 147) for an extra sugar rush.

Makes 10 spoons

1 package (12 ounces/340 g) Wilton Bright White Candy Melts

2 tablespoons finely crushed Oreo cookies (about 2 cookies)

1. Set two 6-spoon silicone spoon moulds on a baking sheet.

2. Place the candy melts in a medium saucepan and melt over low heat, stirring with a rubber spatula until smooth. Stir in the crushed cookies until well blended.

3. Pour the mixture into a squeeze bottle or a pastry bag and divide evenly among 10 of the moulds. Place in the freezer to firm up, about 30 minutes.

4. Remove the spoons by turning the mould upside down and gently pressing them out.

5. Spoons will keep in an airtight container in the refrigerator for up to 1 month.

Overnight Oreo Party Popcorn

This easy recipe is perfect for kids and kids-at-heart alike. The best part is that it can be made the day before your party, so all you have to do is pour it into a bowl and serve.

Makes 8 cups

8 cups popped popcorn
(from about ½ cup kernels)

20 Oreo cookies

1 cup (175 g) white chocolate chips

¼ cup rainbow sprinkles

Sweet Tip

You'll notice while you're mixing the popcorn that it's quite sticky—that's okay. Leaving it to set overnight will take care of that problem, as the popcorn will absorb the moisture and be party-ready.

1. Place the popcorn in a large bowl and set aside.

2. Place the Oreo cookies in a 1-quart resealable plastic bag, seal it and use a rolling pin to roughly crush the cookies. The biggest pieces should be about the size of your thumbnail.

3. Pour the chocolate chips into a microwave-safe bowl. Heat in 15-second intervals, stirring after each interval to prevent the chocolate from burning. Once melted and smooth, set aside to cool slightly.

4. Once the chocolate is cool enough to handle, pour it over the popcorn. With your clean hands (or wearing food-safe disposable gloves), toss the popcorn and chocolate together, making sure to coat as much of the popcorn as possible. Sprinkle with the crushed Oreos (keep the bag) and the rainbow sprinkles and continue mixing, being careful not to crush the popcorn. Once the popcorn is well coated, leave it to cool.

5. Pour the popcorn into the resealable bag you crushed the Oreos in, seal it and allow it to rest at room temperature overnight.

6. Serve in cute individual cups or in a large party bowl. Best eaten the next day, once all the flavours have melded.

Confetti Caramel Popcorn

My first experience with caramel popcorn was at Disneyland when I was nine. I had just had braces put on and wasn't supposed to be eating popcorn at all, let alone popcorn covered in caramel, but I didn't care—this stuff was delicious! My braces are gone now, but my love of this popcorn is just as strong. Use it to top the Carnival Caramel Popcorn Cupcakes (page 71) or serve as a party snack.

Makes 8 cups

8 cups popped popcorn
(from about ½ cup kernels)

1 ½ cups (330 g) packed brown sugar

¾ cup (170 g) unsalted butter,
cut into pieces, room temperature

½ cup light corn syrup

1 teaspoon pure vanilla extract

½ teaspoon baking soda

½ teaspoon salt

¼ cup confetti sprinkles

1. Preheat the oven to 200°F (100°C). Line a baking sheet with parchment paper.

2. Place the popcorn in a large bowl.

3. In a medium saucepan over medium heat, combine the sugar, butter and corn syrup. Allow the ingredients to melt together, stirring occasionally with a wooden spoon. Once melted, let the mixture bubble for about 5 minutes. Remove from the heat and stir in the vanilla, baking soda and salt.

4. Pour the sugar mixture over the popcorn and fold together with a wooden spoon or a rubber spatula. Evenly spread the caramel popcorn on the prepared baking sheet.

5. Bake for 1 hour or until the mixture has thickened and is very sticky, stirring occasionally. Remove the baking sheet from the oven, sprinkle with the confetti sprinkles and stir together with a rubber spatula. Carefully lift the parchment paper with the caramel corn on it off of the baking sheet and place it on the countertop to cool completely.

6. Caramel popcorn will keep in an airtight container for up to 2 weeks.

Vanilla Meringues

These sugary-sweet treats can be tinted every colour of the rainbow, flavoured any which way and even topped with sprinkles. For best results, store them in an airtight container away from moisture.

Makes 20 (2-inch) meringues

White vinegar, for wiping mixer bowl and utensils

4 large egg whites

1 cup (200 g) granulated sugar

Pinch of salt

Pinch of cream of tartar

1 teaspoon pure vanilla extract

2 to 3 drops pink gel food colouring

1 teaspoon edible glitter, for decorating (I use CK) (optional)

Flavour Variations

Cotton Candy: Replace the vanilla extract with 1 teaspoon cotton candy flavouring.

Bubblegum: Replace the vanilla extract with 1 teaspoon bubblegum flavouring.

Watermelon: Replace the vanilla extract with 1 teaspoon watermelon flavouring.

Sprinkle: Instead of using edible glitter, sprinkle ¼ cup nonpareils or confetti sequin sprinkles on the meringues right before they go into the oven.

1. Preheat the oven to 175°F (80°C). Line a baking sheet with parchment paper.

2. Wipe the inside of a mixer bowl, as well as the whisk attachment and a hand whisk, with white vinegar. Pour about 2 inches of water into a medium saucepan and place over medium heat.

3. Place the egg whites and sugar in the mixer bowl and whisk to combine. Place the bowl over the pan of simmering water (but not touching the water) and whisk constantly until the mixture thins and the sugar has dissolved, about 3 to 4 minutes. I usually dip a clean spoon into the mixture and then rub it between my fingers to test whether it's ready. When you can no longer feel any granules of sugar, remove the bowl from the pan.

4. Place the bowl on a stand mixer fitted with the whisk attachment. Add the salt and cream of tartar, then whip on medium-high speed until the meringue has tripled in volume and is thick and glossy. Add the vanilla and whip to combine. Add the food colouring and whip until well blended.

5. Fit a pastry bag with a large French star tip and fill with the meringue mixture. Pipe about twenty 2-inch dollops onto the parchment paper, spacing them apart slightly. (Meringues don't spread, so they can be piped fairly close together.) Sprinkle with the edible glitter, if using.

6. Bake for about 2 hours, until meringues lift easily off of the parchment paper. Allow the meringues to cool completely on the baking sheets.

7. Meringues will keep in an airtight container for up to 2 weeks.

Sweet Tip

Greasy residue (from butter and oils) and egg whites are not friends when making meringues! Fat will prevent your meringue from whipping up into billowy goodness and leave you instead with a soupy mixture. To prevent this, be sure to wipe all bowls and utensils with vinegar, which will get rid of any oily residue.

If you're having trouble with the parchment paper sliding around or rolling up while you're piping your meringues, apply a little bit of the meringue under each corner of the parchment. Press onto the baking sheet, and you're in business.

Mint Chip Cheesecake Cups

These make-ahead treats are an easy and adorable twist on the traditional cheesecake dessert. If your dinner guests are children, serve these with Cookies and Cream Spoons (page 134) for an extra dash of fun.

Makes 6 cheesecake cups

About 12 Oreo cookies

1 package (8 ounces/225 g) full-fat cream cheese, softened

1 cup (125 g) confectioners' sugar

½ cup heavy (35%) cream, cold

1 teaspoon pure peppermint extract

½ teaspoon pure vanilla extract

1 to 2 drops pink gel food colouring

½ cup (90 g) semi-sweet chocolate chips

1 batch Vanilla Bean Whipped Cream (page 199)

Chocolate sprinkles, for decorating (optional)

1. Place 6 small cups, ramekins or jars on a small baking sheet.

2. Finely crush the Oreo cookies in a resealable plastic bag using a rolling pin or pulse in a food processor. You should have 1 cup of crumbs. Divide the crumbs evenly among the cups, pressing flat with the back of a tablespoon or your fingers to form an even base. Set aside.

3. In the bowl of a stand mixer fitted with the whisk attachment, whip the cream cheese until smooth. Add the sugar and cream and whip on medium speed until well blended. Stop the mixer and scrape down the sides of the bowl with a rubber spatula. Add the peppermint and vanilla extracts and the food colouring and whip to blend. Fold in the chocolate chips with a rubber spatula.

4. Divide the batter evenly among the prepared cups and pop the cheesecakes into the refrigerator to chill, at least 5 hours.

5. Right before serving, make the Vanilla Bean Whipped Cream. Fit a pastry bag with a large round piping tip, fill the bag with the whipped cream, then pipe swirls onto the tops of the cheesecakes. Top with sprinkles, if using, and serve immediately.

6. Cheesecakes (without the whipped cream topping) will keep in the refrigerator, covered with plastic wrap, for up to 2 days.

Cookies and Cream Cheesecake Truffle Cups

If pressed to choose between a chocolate or a vanilla dessert, I usually choose vanilla. However, these truffles have been a recent obsession of mine, chocolate and all. The slightly tangy filling balances the sweetness of the chocolate, making this a wonderful treat for those who love something just a little less sweet.

Makes 8 large truffles

3 cups (525 g) semi-sweet chocolate chips

About 6 Oreo cookies

1 package (8 ounces/225 g) full-fat cream cheese, softened

1 cup (125 g) confectioners' sugar

½ cup heavy (35%) cream, cold

Pastel sprinkles, for decorating

1. Place eight 3-inch round silicone moulds or paper cupcake liners on a baking sheet.

2. In a heatproof bowl set over a saucepan of simmering water, melt the chocolate chips, stirring often with a rubber spatula to prevent burning. Remove the bowl from the pan. (Set aside the pan—you'll need it later.)

3. Spoon a few tablespoons of the chocolate into the moulds and use a small food-only paintbrush to draw the chocolate up the sides, making sure to coat them evenly. Place the moulds in the refrigerator to set, about 15 minutes. Set aside the remaining chocolate.

4. While the moulds are setting, finely crush the cookies in a resealable plastic bag using a rolling pin or pulse in a food processor. You should have ½ cup of crumbs.

5. In the bowl of a stand mixer fitted with the whisk attachment, whip the cream cheese until smooth. Add the sugar and cream and whip on medium speed until well blended. Stop the mixer and scrape down the sides and bottom of the bowl with a rubber spatula. Fold in the crushed cookies with the rubber spatula.

6. Divide the mixture evenly among the chocolate moulds, then return them to the refrigerator until just set, about 1 hour.

7. Return the pan of water to a simmer, place the bowl of remaining chocolate over it and melt again. Spoon the melted chocolate over the truffles, smoothing the tops with a small offset spatula. Top with sprinkles. Return the truffles to the refrigerator until set, at least 3 hours or overnight. Just before serving, carefully remove the truffles from the moulds. Serve chilled.

8. Truffle cups will keep in an airtight container in the refrigerator for up to 5 days.

Easy Macaron Ice Cream

Not every dessert needs to be fancy, and sometimes you just don't have the time or the energy. Don't throw away those leftover or broken macarons. Simply fold them into some vanilla ice cream and dessert is served. Scoop into pretty dishes or ice cream cones, or sandwich between two cookies.

Makes 6 to 8 servings

1 tub (2 quarts/2 L) vanilla ice cream

15 macarons, flavours of your choosing, chopped into

1. Place the ice cream in the refrigerator for 5 to 6 hours, or until it is soft enough to be spread.

2. Line the bottom of a 13- × 9-inch baking pan with parchment paper, allowing the parchment to drape over the long sides.

3. Working fairly quickly so the ice cream doesn't start melting, scrape the softened ice cream into a large bowl and fold in the chopped macarons with a rubber spatula. Scrape the ice cream into the prepared pan and spread with an offset spatula or the back of a spoon until even. Cover the top of the pan with plastic wrap, making sure it doesn't touch the ice cream, and place in the freezer until frozen, at least 8 hours or overnight.

4. Serve immediately or cover tightly in plastic wrap and keep in the freezer for up to 1 month.

Sprinkly Chocolate Cake Doughnuts

These baked doughnuts are a healthier alternative to the traditional fried ones and are just as delicious. If you'd prefer a colourful topping, dip them in Sweet Sugar Glaze (page 196) instead of Chocolate Ganache.

Makes 16 doughnuts

DOUGHNUTS

Unsalted butter, for greasing pans

1 cup whole milk, room temperature

¼ cup sour cream

¼ cup vegetable oil

2 large eggs, room temperature

1 teaspoon pure vanilla extract

3 tablespoons (35 g) semi-sweet chocolate chips

1¼ cups (160 g) all-purpose flour, plus more for pans

1 cup (200 g) granulated sugar

¾ cup (85 g) Dutch-processed cocoa powder

1 teaspoon baking soda

½ teaspoon baking powder

½ teaspoon salt

FOR DECORATING

1 batch Chocolate Ganache (page 196)

Pastel sprinkles

1. Preheat the oven to 350°F (180°C). Grease and flour 3 doughnut pans with butter.

2. In a small bowl, whisk together the milk, sour cream, vegetable oil, eggs and vanilla. Set aside.

3. In a heatproof bowl set over a saucepan of simmering water, melt the chocolate chips, stirring often with a rubber spatula to prevent burning. Remove the bowl from the pan and set aside.

4. In the bowl of a stand mixer fitted with the paddle attachment, combine the flour, sugar, cocoa powder, baking soda, baking powder and salt. Mix on low speed to combine. Add the milk mixture and the melted chocolate and mix on low speed to combine. Turn the mixer up to medium speed and beat for about 30 seconds. Stop the mixer and scrape down the sides and bottom of the bowl with a rubber spatula, then mix again on medium speed until well blended, about 10 seconds. Do not over-mix.

5. Pour the batter into a large squeeze bottle or pastry bag and divide evenly among 16 of the doughnut cups, filling each one about halfway. Bake for 15 to 17 minutes, until a toothpick inserted near the centre of the doughnuts comes out clean. Allow the doughnuts to cool in the pans for a few minutes before turning them out onto a wire rack to cool completely.

6. While the doughnuts are cooling, make the Chocolate Ganache. Allow it to cool enough that it thickens slightly. Meanwhile, line a baking sheet with parchment paper and set a wire rack over top.

7. Once the doughnuts have cooled, dip each one top side down into the ganache, then lift it out and allow the excess to drip back into the bowl. Place the doughnut dipped side up on the wire rack. Repeat with the remaining doughnuts. Top with sprinkles.

8. Doughnuts are best eaten on the day that they are baked, but will keep in an airtight container for up to 2 days.

Sugar and Spice Pumpkin Doughnuts

I'm a sucker for a good doughnut, and just because these aren't of the fried variety, it doesn't mean they're any less delicious. Moist and packed with pumpkin, these doughnuts are the perfect snack or breakfast treat.

Makes 18 doughnuts

DOUGHNUTS

Unsalted butter, for greasing pans

2¼ cups plus 1 tablespoon (290 g) all-purpose flour

2 teaspoons baking soda

1 teaspoon baking powder

½ teaspoon salt

2½ teaspoons cinnamon

½ teaspoon ground ginger

¼ teaspoon nutmeg

1¾ cups (350 g) granulated sugar, plus more for tossing the doughnuts

1 cup vegetable oil

4 large eggs, room temperature

1 teaspoon pure vanilla extract

2 cups canned pure pumpkin purée

CINNAMON SUGAR COATING

1 cup (200 g) granulated sugar

2 tablespoons cinnamon

1. Preheat the oven to 350°F (180°C). Grease 3 doughnut pans with butter.

2. In a medium bowl, whisk together the flour, baking soda, baking powder, salt, cinnamon, ginger and nutmeg.

3. In the bowl of a stand mixer fitted with the paddle attachment, beat the sugar, oil, eggs and vanilla on medium speed until blended. Add the flour mixture all at once and mix on low speed until blended. Stop the mixer and scrape down the sides of the bowl with a rubber spatula. Add the pumpkin and mix on low speed until blended, then turn the mixer up to medium speed and beat for 15 seconds. Stop the mixer and scrape down the sides and bottom of the bowl once more, then beat again on medium speed for an additional 15 seconds.

4. Pour the batter into a large squeeze bottle or piping bag and divide evenly among the prepared doughnut pans. Bake for 14 to 17 minutes, until a toothpick inserted into the doughnuts comes out clean. Allow the doughnuts to cool in the pans for 2 minutes before turning them out onto a wire rack to cool slightly.

5. While the doughnuts are cooling, in a medium bowl, whisk together the sugar and cinnamon for the coating.

6. Once the doughnuts are cool enough to handle, toss them in the cinnamon coating, gently pressing each side into the mixture and coating each side evenly. Place the doughnuts back on the wire rack and allow to cool completely.

7. Doughnuts are best eaten on the day that they are baked, but will keep in an airtight container for up to 2 days.

Cookie Dough Scoops

This is the most easy-to-make dessert I've ever created. However, just because it's simple doesn't mean it isn't a crowd-pleaser. If you have kids (or a few girlfriends) coming over, you can whip these up in a pinch and be sure that there won't be a single complaint.

Makes about 18 scoops

1 batch Eggless Chocolate Chip Cookie Dough (page 197)

Pastel sprinkles, for decorating (optional)

1. Line a baking sheet with parchment paper.

2. Make the Eggless Chocolate Chip Cookie Dough. Use an ice cream scoop or two spoons to scoop out balls of the cookie dough and place them on the prepared baking sheet. Top with sprinkles, if desired.

3. Place the scoops in the refrigerator until set, about 30 minutes. Serve chilled.

4. Scoops will keep, covered tightly with plastic wrap in the refrigerator, for up to 5 days.

Frozen Banana Split Cheesecake Cones

My friends' kids love these treats. I took them to a birthday party one summer and everyone went nuts! This dessert is a refreshing alternative to ice cream and can be decorated with anything your heart desires—crushed cookies, macarons, nuts, rainbow sprinkles, you name it.

Makes 10 cones

FOR CHEESECAKE CONES

10 ice cream cones

1 package (8 ounces/225 g) full-fat cream cheese, softened

1 cup (125 g) confectioners' sugar

¾ cup heavy (35%) cream, cold

1 ripe medium banana, mashed

½ teaspoon pure vanilla extract

FOR DECORATING

1 batch Vanilla Bean Whipped Cream (page 199)

1 drop pink gel food colouring

Chocolate sprinkles

10 maraschino cherries

1. Place an ice cream cone holder (or 10 drinking glasses) on a baking sheet and set a cone in each one.

2. In the bowl of a stand mixer filled with the whisk attachment, whip the cream cheese until smooth. Add the sugar and cream and whip on medium speed until well blended. Stop the mixer and scrape down the sides of the bowl with a rubber spatula. Add the mashed banana and the vanilla and whip to blend.

3. Divide the batter evenly among the cones. Pop them into the freezer to firm up, at least 5 hours.

4. Right before serving, make the Vanilla Bean Whipped Cream. Once it has finished whipping, add the pink food colouring and whip to combine.

5. Fit a pastry bag with a large piping tip, fill the bag with the whipped cream, then pipe swirls onto the tops of the cheesecakes. Top with sprinkles and finish with a cherry. Serve immediately.

6. Cheesecakes (without the decoration) will keep in an airtight container in the freezer for up to 5 days.

Macaron Fudge

I'm continuously searching for new ways to use broken or extra macarons—throwing them away would be tragic. Folding them into fudge just seemed like a good idea. The melt-in-your-mouth texture of the fudge combined with chewy bits of macaron makes this dessert one of my all-time favourites.

Makes 16 pieces

2 teaspoons unsalted butter, room temperature

1 teaspoon pure vanilla extract

2¾ cups (550 g) granulated sugar

1¼ cups heavy (35%) cream

2 tablespoons plus 1 teaspoon light corn syrup

8 macarons, flavours of your choosing, chopped into pieces

1. Line the bottom of an 8- × 8-inch baking dish with parchment paper.

2. Place the butter and vanilla in the bowl of a stand mixer and set aside.

3. In a medium saucepan, stir together the sugar, cream and corn syrup. Place over medium-low heat and stir occasionally until the sugar has completely dissolved, 10 to 12 minutes.

4. Turn the heat up slightly and clip a candy thermometer onto the side of the pan (or use an infrared thermometer). Allow the mixture to bubble gently, without stirring, until the temperature reaches 238°F (115°C).

5. Carefully pour the sugar mixture into the mixer bowl with the butter and vanilla. Do not scrape the excess mixture out of the saucepan. Allow the mixture to cool in the bowl, without stirring, until it reaches 115°F (45°C), about 90 minutes.

6. Once the mixture is ready, transfer the bowl to a stand mixer fitted with the paddle attachment. Stir on low speed until the mixture begins to thicken and loses its gloss, 2 to 3 minutes. Fold in the chopped macarons with a rubber spatula, then scrape the mixture into the prepared baking dish. Smooth with a spatula or the back of a spoon. Transfer the baking dish to the refrigerator and chill until the fudge is firm, 6 to 8 hours.

7. Once the fudge is firm, run a sharp knife along the edges, loosening it from the baking dish. Use an offset spatula to gently lift out the fudge. Cut into 2-inch squares.

8. Fudge will keep in an airtight container in the refrigerator for up to 1 week.

Cookie Dough Truffles

These truffles are the perfect treat for any chocolate lover. Placed in pretty boxes, they make lovely gifts. For the most delicious results, use high-quality chocolate.

Makes 12 truffles

1 batch Eggless Peanut Butter Cookie Dough (page 198)

7 cups (1.2 kg) semi-sweet chocolate chips

Rainbow sprinkles, for decorating

1. Place a silicone chocolate mould containing twelve 3- × 1-inch rectangle moulds on a small baking sheet lined with parchment paper.

2. Make the Eggless Peanut Butter Cookie Dough and set aside.

3. In a heatproof bowl set over a saucepan of simmering water, melt the chocolate chips, stirring often with a rubber spatula to prevent burning. Pour the melted chocolate into a large plastic squeeze bottle.

4. Squeeze the melted chocolate into the mould, filling each mould about one-third full. Scoop out a heaping tablespoon of cookie dough, roll it into a log and place it gently in the centre of one of the moulds, on top of the melted chocolate. Make sure that the dough doesn't touch the sides of the mould or extend above the height of the mould. There will be extra cookie dough left over – simply store in an airtight container for another time. Squeeze more of the melted chocolate around and on top of the cookie dough, filling the mould to the top. Smooth over with the back of a table knife. Repeat with the remaining moulds.

5. Transfer the truffles to the freezer and allow to set completely, about 20 minutes.

6. Remove the truffles by turning the mould upside down and gently pressing them out. Place the truffles on the baking sheet, right side up. Drizzle the remaining chocolate over the top of each truffle, then finish with sprinkles. Return the truffles to the freezer for an additional 10 minutes to set.

7. Truffles will keep in an airtight container in the refrigerator for up to 5 days.

Sparkles and Sprinkles Cookie Bark

One of my favourite things to serve at holiday parties is chocolate bark. It's easy to make and is a treat that my friends all love. The best part about bark is that you can flavour it any which way, by adding any extracts and toppings of your choosing, depending on what you're craving.

Makes one 12-inch-square slab of bark

2 packages (12 ounces/340 g each) Wilton Bright White Candy Melts

½ teaspoon peppermint extract

1 to 2 drops pink gel food colouring

¼ cup crushed Oreo cookies (about 4 cookies) or cookie of choice

Multicoloured sprinkles, for decorating

Edible glitter, for decorating (I use CK)

1. Line a baking sheet with parchment paper.

2. Place the candy melts in a medium saucepan and melt over low heat, stirring with a rubber spatula until smooth. Stir in the peppermint extract until well blended.

3. Divide the melted chocolate between two bowls. Stir the food colouring into one bowl until blended.

4. Pour both bowls of chocolate onto the prepared baking sheet and use the handle of a spoon to swirl the two colours together, creating a marbled effect. Sprinkle with the crushed cookies, multicoloured sprinkles and edible glitter.

5. Place the bark in the refrigerator until set, about 30 minutes. Break apart by hand before serving or storing.

6. Bark will keep in an airtight container in the refrigerator for up to 1 month.

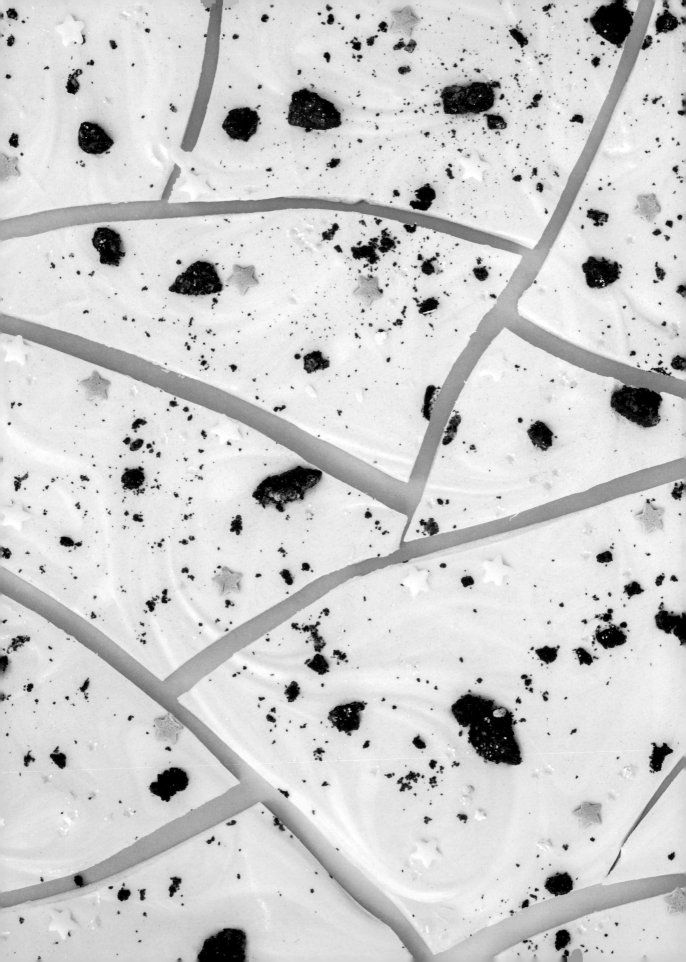

Sprinkly Nanaimo Bars

I grew up in a small town on Vancouver Island, on the west coast of Canada, about three hours' drive from the city of Nanaimo. So naturally, I've had a few Nanaimo bars in my life! Traditionally, the filling in the middle of these bars is yellow, but because pink is my favourite colour, that's the colour I chose for mine. Top with sprinkles for a pop of colour.

Makes 9 bars

CRUST

1 large egg, cold

½ cup (115 g) unsalted butter, room temperature

½ cup (55 g) Dutch-processed cocoa powder

3 tablespoons (40 g) granulated sugar

1½ cups graham cracker crumbs

1¼ cups unsweetened shredded coconut

FILLING

½ cup (115 g) unsalted butter, room temperature

¼ cup heavy (35%) cream, room temperature

2 tablespoons custard powder

2 teaspoons pure vanilla extract

2¼ cups (280 g) confectioners' sugar

1 to 2 drops pink gel food colouring

TOPPING

2 cups (350 g) semi-sweet chocolate chips

2 tablespoons (30 g) unsalted butter, room temperature

Multicoloured sprinkles, for decorating

1. Line the bottom of an 8-inch square cake pan with parchment paper.

2. Make the crust: In a medium bowl, beat the egg with a fork; set aside. In a heatproof bowl set over a saucepan of simmering water, combine the butter, cocoa powder and sugar. Stir constantly until the mixture is melted and smooth. Whisk the mixture into the egg, in three portions, whisking constantly to avoid curdling the egg. Fold in the graham cracker crumbs and coconut until blended. Press the mixture into the bottom of the prepared cake pan and set aside.

3. Make the filling: In the bowl of a stand mixer fitted with the paddle attachment, beat the butter on medium speed until smooth and creamy. Add the cream, custard powder and vanilla and beat on medium speed until blended. Add the confectioners' sugar and mix on low speed until combined. Stop the mixer and scrape down the sides of the bowl with a rubber spatula. Add the food colouring, then beat on medium speed until smooth, about 30 seconds. Pour over the crust in the prepared pan and spread out in an even layer. Place in the refrigerator until set, about 30 minutes.

4. Make the topping: Place the chocolate chips and the butter in a heatproof bowl. Set over a saucepan of simmering water and melt, stirring often with a rubber spatula to prevent burning. Pour the melted chocolate over the set filling. Use an offset spatula to smooth the topping, and then sprinkle with the multicoloured sprinkles. Chill in the refrigerator until set, about 1 hour. Cut into 9 bars using a sharp knife.

5. Bars will keep in the refrigerator, covered with plastic wrap or in an airtight container, for up to 5 days.

Marvellous Macarons

French Macarons: Important Things to Remember

Macarons can be incredibly fussy and kind of tricky to make, especially if you're new to making them. However, once you learn where you went wrong, you'll know how to avoid the problem. Just like anything else, practice makes perfect.

1. Weighing your ingredients is key. Investing in an inexpensive digital scale will help prevent over- or under-measuring your ingredients. I swear by weighing my macaron ingredients, always.

2. Ridding your bowls and utensils of any greasy residue is crucial. By wiping everything with vinegar, you're eliminating the possibility of your egg whites not whipping up properly. Improperly whipped egg whites will result in failed macarons.

3. Learning proper folding and mixing makes all the difference. It can take a few batches to really get the hang of the proper folding techniques and to spot the perfect batter consistency. It took me at least three batches of really messing things up to finally get my macarons looking right.

4. Every oven is different, and what works in my oven may not work in yours. All ovens have hot spots, where things cook very quickly. Purchasing a few inexpensive oven thermometers can help you figure this out easily. You will most likely have to adjust your oven temperature a little bit while making macarons and find out what works just right for you. You'll find that rotating the baking sheets and shuffling them onto different racks during the baking process will help your macarons bake evenly and without issue.

French Macaron Troubleshooting Tips

These are the most common problems I've had in all my years of making macarons, followed by what I found to be the best solutions.

1. **Macarons spread/flatten completely after piping** The batter has been over-mixed and has been deflated. Next time, mix the batter less, stopping once it reaches the gentle lava-like consistency.

2. **Lopsided macarons** The fan or convection was too high, or possibly your baking sheet is warped. Next time, turn off the convection and add a few minutes to the baking time. Don't use warped baking sheets for making macarons.

3. **Lumpy macarons** The ingredients were not sifted or the batter was not mixed enough. Next time, be sure to sift the ingredients and properly mix the batter.

4. **Wet bottom that sticks to your mat** The macarons are under-baked. Try baking longer or increasing your oven temperature next time.

5. **Bottom that is concave and doesn't stick to the mat** The batter was over-mixed. Next time, mix the batter less, stopping once it reaches the gentle lava-like consistency.

6. **Points or peaks on your macarons** The batter was not mixed enough. Next time, mix the batter until it flows gently, like lava. Also, after piping the macarons, be sure to rap the baking sheet on the counter several times to help remove air bubbles and smooth them out.

7. **Hollow shells** The shells could be slightly under-baked. Try adding a few minutes to your baking time or lifting up the silicone mat and gently turning it upside down with the macarons still attached while cooling. Another cause could be improper whipping of egg whites—be sure to whip them until stiff, but not dried-out, peaks form.

8. **Very large feet** The oven temperature was too high or the baking sheet was in a hot spot for too long. Try reducing the temperature or moving the baking sheet to another spot in the oven.

9. **Top of macarons are browned** The oven temperature may be too high or the macarons may be in a hot spot. Try reducing the temperature and adding a few minutes to the baking time, or loosely cover the macarons with aluminum foil, which can shield them from the heat.

Basic French Macarons

In my kitchen, I use the "French method" of making macarons, as opposed to the "Italian method" or "Swiss method." Almost every baker I've ever met has sworn by one method over the other, but in my opinion, all three produce wonderful results. I prefer the French method because I cannot be trusted around a pot of hot, bubbling ingredients.

Some bakers swear by aging their egg whites for macarons, which involves keeping the egg whites in an airtight container for at least 24 hours before using them. They say that this process reduces moisture content and increases elasticity.

Other bakers swear by using fresh egg whites, separated from the yolks and used right away. I'm with this group, for two reasons: first, it works for me and my recipes, and second, I don't want to have to prepare my egg whites in advance. What if I need to make macarons right away? What if I mess up a batch and have no more aged egg whites left? Madness, I tell you.

There is also a healthy debate about whether you should bake macarons on parchment paper or silicone macaron mats. I prefer to use silicone mats—I mean the ones with templates for the macarons, not simply nonstick baking mats—because they never wrinkle like parchment paper can, and you can reuse them over and over again. They take a little getting used to when it comes to lifting the macarons off them, but I recommend using them. Of course, to each their own.

When you're learning to make macarons, it's inevitable that you'll mess up a few times, and that's okay! It's all part of the learning process, and you'll definitely learn a thing or two with every batch. You can take comfort in knowing that I've messed up many times too. See my French Macaron Troubleshooting Tips (page 167) to help you out.

Makes 32 shells

White vinegar, for wiping mixer bowl and whisk attachment

1 ¼ cups plus 2 tablespoons (175 g) confectioners' sugar

¾ cup plus 3 tablespoons (105 g) almond flour

2 teaspoons (6 g) canola oil

3 fresh egg whites (90 g)

¼ cup plus 2 tablespoons (75 g) granulated sugar

1 to 2 drops gel food colouring (optional)

Sprinkles (optional)

1. Line two baking sheets with silicone macaron mats or parchment paper with circle guides (see page 206 for templates).

2. Wipe the inside of a mixer bowl, as well as the whisk attachment, with white vinegar.

3. Fit a pastry bag with a plain piping tip (I use a Wilton #12 tip for macarons).

4. In the bowl of a food processor, combine the confectioners' sugar, almond flour and canola oil. Process for 30 seconds, or until well blended. Sift the ingredients onto a sheet of parchment paper, then pour them into a bowl and set aside.

5. Place the egg whites and the granulated sugar in the prepared mixer bowl. Attach the bowl, as well as the whip attachment, to the stand mixer. Beat on medium-low speed until the mixture becomes opaque (SEE PHOTO 1, page 170), about 3 minutes. Turn the mixer up to medium and beat until the meringue has gained volume (SEE PHOTO 2, page 170), about 2 minutes. Lastly, turn the mixer up to medium-high and beat until the meringue holds stiff peaks and is the consistency of shaving cream (SEE PHOTO 3, page 170), 2 to 3 minutes. Add the gel food colouring, if using, and beat until just combined.

6. Remove the bowl from the mixer and scrape down the whisk attachment with a rubber spatula to remove any clinging meringue. Fold in half of the almond mixture with the rubber spatula, using the "fold and smear" technique (SEE PHOTOS 4 AND 5, page 170). This will blend the batter together while deflating it slightly. Be sure to scrape the spatula on the rim of the bowl often, to prevent clumps from forming. Add the remaining almond mixture and fold in using the same technique. Continue to fold until the batter has deflated and has become softer, but be careful not to over-mix. Test its readiness by drizzling a ribbon of batter back over itself—it should flow gently like lava and almost fully disappear in about 30 seconds (SEE PHOTO 6, page 170). If the ribbon is still visible after 30 seconds, the batter needs to be folded slightly more. If the ribbon disappears too quickly, the batter has been over-mixed and you'll need to start over.

7. Fill the prepared pastry bag with the batter. Holding the bag upright, with the tip about ½ inch above the mat and in the centre of one of the circles, squeeze out the batter, stopping just before it reaches the inside edge of the circle.

8. Once all the macarons are piped, carefully rap the baking sheet on the countertop several times, which will help to get rid of any air bubbles. Add the sprinkles, if using. Allow the piped macarons to rest at room temperature until they develop a "skin" that does not stick to your finger, 25 to 30 minutes.

9. While the macarons are resting, preheat the oven to 325°F (160°C) and position the racks in the middle of the oven. Tear off two sheets of aluminum foil roughly the same size as the baking sheets.

10. After 30 minutes, turn the temperature down to 300°F (150°C) and place the macarons in the oven. Bake for 9 minutes, then rotate the baking sheets front to back and top to bottom. Bake for

another 8 minutes. Open the oven door and carefully place the foil sheets, shiny side up, over the macarons to help prevent browning or discoloration. Bake for 8 more minutes, then remove the macarons from the oven. To test doneness, gently place the pad of your index finger on top of one of the macarons and wiggle slightly. If the macaron slides or moves, it needs a minute or two more. If it doesn't move, the macarons are ready to be taken out. Carefully remove the foil and allow the macarons to cool completely on the baking sheets.

11. Remove the macarons from the baking sheets by gently and slowly lifting them off the silicone mat or parchment paper. Sometimes it helps to lift the mat and peel it away from the macarons.

12. Gently place the macaron shells in an airtight container or a resealable plastic bag. Macarons will keep in a resealable plastic bag in the refrigerator for up to 2 days or in a resealable plastic bag in an airtight container in the freezer for up to 3 months.

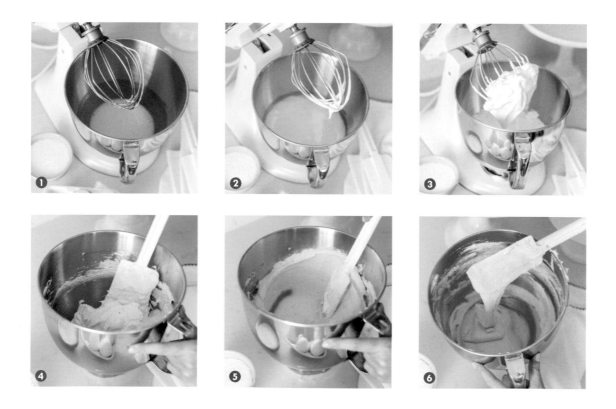

Pink Coconut Macarons

Pink is a favourite colour of mine (not sure if you could tell!), so when I stumbled upon pink shredded coconut while grocery shopping, I knew it had to come home with me. Try stirring ¼ cup of Wonderful Caramel (page 200) into the coconut frosting for a delightful flavour combination.

Makes 32 shells or 16 macarons

1 batch Basic French Macarons (page 168)

½ cup shredded pink coconut

1 batch Bake Shop Vanilla Frosting (page 190)

1 to 2 teaspoons coconut flavouring or extract

1 to 2 drops pink gel food colouring

1. Make the Basic French Macarons, sprinkling with the coconut in step 8. Bake as directed, allow to cool completely, then remove from the baking sheets.

2. Make the Bake Shop Vanilla Frosting, adding the coconut flavouring and pink food colouring along with the vanilla. Fit a pastry bag with a plain piping tip and half fill with the frosting. Pipe a dollop of frosting onto the underside of one of the macaron shells. Sandwich its matching shell on top so that the bottom of each shell is against the frosting.

3. Place the filled macarons in an airtight container or resealable plastic bag and pop into the refrigerator. Leave them to rest in the refrigerator for at least 12 hours before serving, to allow the moisture from the filling to meld together with the shells, creating optimum texture. Allow the macarons to come to room temperature on a baking sheet for about 2 hours before serving.

4. Filled macarons will keep in a resealable plastic bag in the refrigerator for up to 2 days or in a resealable bag in an airtight container in the freezer for up to 1 month. Unfilled shells will keep in the freezer, in a resealable bag placed in an airtight container, for up to 3 months.

Oreo Cheesecake Macarons

Cream cheese and Oreos unite to create a distinct and not-too-sweet filling that will please dessert lovers every-where. Eat the macarons as is, or chop them up and fold them into the Easy Macaron Ice Cream (page 147) for a chilly treat.

Makes 32 shells or 16 macarons

About 3 Oreo cookies

1 batch Basic French Macarons
(page 168)

1 to 2 drops purple gel food colouring

1 batch Cream Cheese Frosting
(page 191), Oreo variation

1. Place the Oreos in a resealable plastic bag and use a rolling pin to finely crush them. You should have ¼ cup crumbs. Set aside.

2. Make the Basic French Macarons, adding the food colouring at the end of step 5 and sprinkling with the Oreo crumbs in step 8. Bake as directed, allow to cool completely, then remove from the baking sheets.

3. Make the Oreo Cream Cheese Frosting. Fit a pastry bag with a plain piping tip and half fill with the frosting. Pipe a dollop onto the underside of one of the macaron shells. Sandwich its matching shell on top so that the bottom of each macaron shell is against the frosting.

4. Place the filled macarons in an airtight container or resealable plastic bag and pop into the refrigerator. Leave them to rest in the refrigerator for at least 12 hours before serving, to allow the moisture from the filling to meld together with the shells, creating optimum texture. Allow the macarons to come to room temperature on a baking sheet for about 2 hours before serving.

5. Filled macarons will keep in a resealable plastic bag in the refrigerator for up to 2 days or in a resealable plastic bag in an airtight container in the freezer for up to 1 month. Unfilled shells will keep in the freezer, in a resealable bag placed in an airtight container, for up to 3 months.

24 Karat Vanilla Macarons

These macarons are always eye-catching, yet they are so simple to decorate! They were easily the most requested macaron on our menu and look stunning piled on a plate or packaged individually as favours.

Makes 32 shells or 16 macarons

1 batch Basic French Macarons (page 168)

Cold food paint (or gold lustre dust mixed with 1 teaspoon clear alcohol such as vodka or gin)

1 batch Bake Shop Vanilla Frosting (page 190)

1. Make the Basic French Macarons. Allow the macarons to cool completely on the baking sheets.

2. Line another baking sheet with parchment paper. Remove the macarons from the baking sheets by gently and slowly lifting them off the silicone mat or parchment paper. Sometimes it helps to lift the mat and peel it away from the macarons. Place the macarons on the prepared baking sheet.

3. Dip a food-only paintbrush into the gold food paint and use your finger to flick the gold off the bristles and onto the macarons, creating a speckled effect. Allow the paint to dry completely. Once dry, match each macaron shell with another of the same size, placing the two shells together.

4. Make the Bake Shop Vanilla Frosting. Fit a pastry bag with a plain piping tip and half fill with the frosting. Pipe a dollop of frosting onto the underside of one of the macaron shells. Sandwich its matching shell on top so that the bottom of each shell is against the frosting.

5. Place the filled macarons in an airtight container or resealable plastic bag and pop into the refrigerator. Leave them to rest in the refrigerator for at least 12 hours before serving, to allow the moisture from the filling to meld together with the shells, creating optimum texture. Allow the macarons to come to room temperature on a baking sheet for about 2 hours before serving.

6. Filled macarons will keep in a resealable plastic bag in the refrigerator for up to 2 days or in a resealable plastic bag in an airtight container in the freezer for up to 1 month. Unfilled shells will keep in the freezer, in a resealable bag placed in an airtight container, for up to 3 months.

Fuzzy Peach Macarons

Named after the famous candy, these peachy, sugar-coated macarons are one of my most-requested desserts. For a more authentic peach look, tuck pieces of green food-grade paper into the edges.

Makes 32 shells or 16 macarons

1 batch Basic French Macarons (page 168)

2 to 4 drops orange gel food colouring, divided

¼ cup water

1 small drop red gel food colouring

1 cup (200 g) granulated sugar

1 batch Bake Shop Vanilla Frosting (page 190)

2 to 3 teaspoons peach flavouring (I use LorAnn Oils)

1. Make the Basic French Macarons, adding 1 to 2 drops of orange food colouring at the end of step 5. Bake as directed and allow the macarons to cool completely on the baking sheets.

2. Line another baking sheet with parchment paper. Remove the macarons from the baking sheets by gently and slowly lifting them off the silicone mat or parchment paper. Sometimes it helps to lift the mat and peel it away from the macarons. Place the macarons on the prepared baking sheet.

3. Place the water and red food colouring in a small bowl and stir to blend. Using a pastry brush, lightly coat the top of each macaron with the tinted water, then immediately sprinkle some of the sugar over top. Allow the macarons to dry completely, about 1 hour.

4. Make the Bake Shop Vanilla Frosting, adding the remaining 1 to 2 drops of orange food colouring and the peach flavouring along with the vanilla. Fit a pastry bag with a plain piping tip and half fill with the frosting. Pipe a dollop of frosting onto the underside of one of the macaron shells. Sandwich its matching shell on top so that the bottom of each macaron shell is against the frosting.

5. Place the filled macarons in an airtight container or resealable plastic bag and pop into the refrigerator. Leave them to rest in the refrigerator for at least 12 hours before serving, to allow the moisture from the filling to meld together with the shells, creating optimum texture. Allow the macarons to come to room temperature on a baking sheet for about 2 hours before serving.

6. Filled macarons will keep in a resealable plastic bag in the refrigerator for up to 2 days or in a resealable bag in an airtight container in the freezer for up to 1 month. Unfilled shells will keep in the freezer, in a resealable plastic bag placed in an airtight container, for up to 3 months.

Cookie Dough Sprinkle Macarons

If you love cookie dough as much as I do, these macarons are for you. You will most likely have extra dough left over after filling the shells, but that's okay! You can store it in the refrigerator for later or simply grab a spoon and eat to your heart's content.

Makes 32 shells or 16 macarons

1 batch Basic French Macarons
(page 168)

1 to 2 drops blue gel food colouring

Rainbow sprinkles

1 batch Eggless Chocolate Chip Cookie
Dough (page 197)

Sweet Tip

Sometimes it can be a bit difficult to pipe the cookie dough, because of the chocolate chips. To make things easier, roughly chop the chocolate chips (or pulse them in a food processor) to make them a bit smaller, then stir them into the dough.

1. Make the Basic French Macarons, adding the food colouring at the end of step 5 and topping with the sprinkles in step 8. Bake as directed, allow to cool completely, then remove from the baking sheets.

2. Make the Eggless Chocolate Chip Cookie Dough. Fit a pastry bag with a large plain piping tip and half fill with the dough. Pipe a dollop of cookie dough onto the underside of one of the macaron shells. Sandwich its matching shell on top so that the bottom of each macaron shell is against the filling.

3. Place the filled macarons in an airtight container or resealable plastic bag and pop into the refrigerator. Leave them to rest in the refrigerator for at least 12 hours before serving, to allow the moisture from the filling to meld together with the shells, creating optimum texture. Allow the macarons to come to room temperature on a baking sheet for about 2 hours before serving.

4. Filled macarons will keep in a resealable plastic bag in the refrigerator for up to 2 days or in a resealable plastic bag in an airtight container in the freezer for up to 1 month. Unfilled shells will keep in the freezer, in a resealable bag placed in an airtight container, for up to 3 months.

Birthday Cake Macarons

These macarons are ready to party! Filled with birthday cake goodness and topped with sprinkles, they make the perfect party-time treat.

Makes 32 shells or 16 macarons

1 batch Basic French Macarons (page 168)

Rainbow sprinkles

1 batch Cake Batter Frosting (page 193)

1 to 2 drops pink gel food colouring

1. Make the Basic French Macarons, topping with the sprinkles in step 8. Bake as directed, allow to cool completely, then remove from the baking sheets.

2. Make the Cake Batter Frosting, adding the food colouring with the vanilla. Fit a pastry bag with a plain piping tip and half fill with the frosting. Pipe a dollop of frosting onto the underside of one of the macaron shells. Sandwich its matching shell on top so that the bottom of each macaron shell is against the frosting.

3. Place the filled macarons in an airtight container or resealable plastic bag and pop into the refrigerator. Leave them to rest in the refrigerator for at least 12 hours before serving, to allow the moisture from the filling to meld together with the shells, creating optimum texture. Allow the macarons to come to room temperature on a baking sheet for about 2 hours before serving.

4. Filled macarons will keep in a resealable plastic bag in the refrigerator for up to 2 days or in a resealable plastic bag in an airtight container in the freezer for up to 1 month. Unfilled shells will keep in the freezer, in a resealable bag placed in an airtight container, for up to 3 months.

Cotton Candy Cloud Macarons

Filled with sweet frosting and decorated daintily, these macarons were one of the most darling desserts we made. Packaged individually, they make the perfect take-home party treats.

Makes 10 shells or 5 macarons

1 batch Basic French Macarons batter (page 168)

Black food decorating pen or fine-tip edible marker

Pink lustre dust (I use CK)

1 batch Bake Shop Vanilla Frosting, cotton candy variation (page 190)

1 to 2 drops turquoise gel food colouring

1. Cut two sheets of parchment paper to fit two baking sheets. Trace five clouds onto each sheet of parchment, using the templates on page 206 and a food decorating pen. Place one sheet of parchment on each baking sheet, then place a silicone baking mat over top. You should be able to see your templates through the mats.

2. Make the Basic French Macarons batter (steps 2 through 6).

3. Fill the prepared pastry bag with the batter. Hold it upright over one of the baking sheets, with the tip about ½ inch above the mat, and squeeze the batter into the middle of each one of the circles, following the numbers 1 through 5 in sequence. Stop just before the batter reaches the inside edge of each circle. Use a toothpick or the tip of a knife to push together the batter and fill any small gaps in the cloud shapes.

4. Once the macarons are piped, rap the baking sheets on the countertop several times to remove any air bubbles. Allow the piped macarons to rest at room temperature until they develop a "skin" that does not stick to your finger, 25 to 30 minutes.

5. While the macarons are resting, preheat the oven to 325°F (160°C). Tear off two sheets of aluminum foil roughly the same size as the baking sheets, and set aside.

6. After 30 minutes, turn the temperature down to 300°F (150°C) and place the macarons in the oven. Bake for 9 minutes, then rotate the baking sheets front to back and top to bottom. Bake for another 8 minutes. Open the oven door and carefully place the foil sheets, shiny side up, over the macarons to help prevent any browning or discoloration. Bake for 10 more minutes, then remove the macarons from the oven. Carefully remove the foil and allow the macarons to cool completely on the baking sheets.

7. Remove the macarons from the baking sheets by gently and slowly lifting them off the silicone mat or parchment paper. Sometimes it helps to lift the mat and peel it away from the macarons.

8. Match each cloud with another of the same size, placing the two shells together. Use the black food decorating pen to draw eyelashes and a smile on one macaron from each pair. Dip a small food-only paintbrush into the lustre dust, tap off the excess and sweep blushed cheeks onto each side of the smile.

9. Make the Cotton Candy Frosting, adding the food colouring with the vanilla. Fit a large pastry bag with a large round piping tip and half fill with the frosting. Pipe frosting onto the undersides of five of the macarons, then gently sandwich together with their matching macarons.

10. Place the filled macarons in an airtight container or resealable plastic bag and pop into the refrigerator. Leave them to rest in the refrigerator for at least 12 hours before serving, to allow the moisture from the filling to meld together with the shells, creating optimum texture. Allow the macarons to come to room temperature on a baking sheet for about 2 hours before serving.

11. Filled macarons will keep in a resealable plastic bag in the refrigerator for up to 2 days or in a resealable plastic bag in an airtight container in the freezer for up to 1 month. Unfilled shells will keep in the freezer, in a resealable bag placed in an airtight container, for up to 3 months.

Sweet Tip

If you won't be using silicone baking mats, be sure to flip the parchment paper over on your baking sheet, so the traced templates are on the bottom. That way, you'll avoid any transfer of the ink to your macarons while baking.

Frostings and Fillings

Bake Shop Vanilla Frosting

Every baker has a basic vanilla frosting that they love enough to fill and decorate their desserts. Mine is made with vanilla bean paste, but using vanilla extract is just fine, too! This frosting can be flavoured almost any which way, simply by adding your favourite extract, spread or whatever your heart desires. Use it to frost Vanilla Birthday Cake (page 28), pipe swirls onto French Cupcakes (page 60) and more.

Makes 4 cups

2 cups (450 g) unsalted butter, room temperature

4½ cups (560 g) confectioners' sugar

2 teaspoons vanilla bean paste
(or 1 teaspoon pure vanilla extract)

1. In the bowl of a stand mixer fitted with the paddle attachment, beat the butter on medium speed until creamy, about 30 seconds.

2. With the mixer running on low speed, gradually add the sugar, 1 cup at a time, until incorporated. Turn the mixer up to medium speed and beat for about 2 minutes, until the frosting is light and fluffy. Stop the mixer and scrape down the sides and bottom of the bowl with a rubber spatula.

3. Add the vanilla, then beat on medium speed for 1 additional minute.

4. Use immediately to frost cakes, cupcakes and more.

Flavour Variations

Caramel Frosting: Add ¼ cup caramel with the vanilla.

Chocolate Frosting: Add 2 tablespoons chocolate ganache and ⅓ cup (40 g) cocoa powder with the vanilla.

Cinnamon Frosting: Add 1 to 2 tablespoons cinnamon with the vanilla.

Cookies and Cream Frosting: Add 1 cup finely crushed Oreo cookies (about 12 cookies) with the vanilla.

Cotton Candy Frosting: Add 1 teaspoon cotton candy flavouring with the vanilla.

Peanut Butter Frosting: Add ¼ cup smooth peanut butter with the vanilla.

Peppermint Frosting: Add 1 teaspoon peppermint extract with the vanilla.

Pink Lemonade Frosting: Add 2 to 3 teaspoons lemon or lemonade drink powder with the vanilla.

Cream Cheese Frosting

This light, fluffy frosting is just the right amount of sweet. It pipes onto the Red Velvet Cupcakes (page 85) like a dream and covers cakes, like the Red Velvet Oreo Sprinkle Cake (page 32), beautifully and with ease.

Makes 5 cups

2 cups (450 g) unsalted butter, room temperature

½ cup (110 g) cream cheese, softened

5½ cups (700 g) confectioners' sugar

1 teaspoon pure vanilla extract

1. In the bowl of a stand mixer fitted with the paddle attachment, beat together the butter and cream cheese on medium speed until smooth. Stop the mixer and scrape down the sides and bottom of the bowl with a rubber spatula.

2. With the mixer running on low speed, gradually add the confectioners' sugar. Add the vanilla, then turn the mixer up to medium speed and beat until light and fluffy, about 2 minutes. Stop the mixer and scrape down the sides and bottom of the bowl, then beat again on medium speed again for 15 seconds.

3. Use immediately or store in the refrigerator in an airtight container for up to 2 days. To return to a smooth consistency, allow the frosting to sit at room temperature, uncovered, for 30 minutes, then beat on medium speed until smooth.

Flavour Variations

Caramel Cream Cheese Frosting: Add 2 to 3 tablespoons caramel with the vanilla.

Cinnamon Cream Cheese Frosting: Add 1 to 2 teaspoons cinnamon with the vanilla.

Lemon Cream Cheese Frosting: Add 2 to 3 teaspoons pure lemon extract with the vanilla.

Oreo Cream Cheese Frosting: Add ½ cup to 1 cup finely crushed Oreo cookies (6 to 12 cookies) with the vanilla.

Dreamy Marshmallow Frosting

I dream about this frosting. Its super-light texture and delicate sweetness make it a perfect finish on cakes and cupcakes that command full attention. Not only does it brown up nicely when torched, like with the Summer Party Cake (page 40) and Summertime S'more Cupcakes (page 68), but it also takes food colouring like a dream. Because this is a meringue-based frosting, you must use it immediately. Otherwise, you'll be left with a sweet, sticky mess.

Makes 2½ cups

White vinegar, for wiping mixer bowl and utensils

3 large egg whites

¾ cup (150 g) granulated sugar

1¼ teaspoons light corn syrup

½ teaspoon pure vanilla extract

Pinch of cream of tartar

Pinch of salt

1. Wipe the inside of a mixer bowl, as well as the whisk attachment and a hand whisk, with white vinegar. Pour about 2 inches of water into a medium saucepan and place over medium heat.

2. Separate the egg whites from the yolks. Set the yolks aside for another use or discard.

3. Place the egg whites, sugar and corn syrup in the mixer bowl and whisk to combine. Place the bowl over the pan of simmering water (but not touching the water) and whisk constantly until the mixture is warm to the touch and no longer feels grainy when rubbed between your thumb and forefinger, about 3 to 4 minutes.

4. Attach the bowl to a stand mixer fitted with the whisk attachment and add the vanilla, cream of tartar and salt. Whip on medium-high speed until the mixture has tripled in volume and is thick and glossy white. Stop the mixer and add flavouring or food colouring, if using, and whip until just combined.

5. Use immediately.

Sweet Tip

If you're wondering what this "wipe the bowl with vinegar" business is all about, allow me to explain. Oil and egg whites aren't friends, but only when the egg whites need to whip into a meringue. Oily residue (from butter or vegetable oil, for example) prevents the egg whites from whipping up into a fluffy dream, which will waste not only your time but your ingredients, as you'll have to dump them out and begin again. Frustrating, yes, but preventable. Be sure to wipe your bowl and all utensils well, and you're in business.

Cake Batter Frosting

As much as I love a vanilla cake made from scratch, there's something about the flavour of the store-bought version that I really enjoy. The cake mix in this recipe really brings the frosting to sweet, sugary life. It pairs perfectly with Dreamy Vanilla Cake (page 19) and Sprinkly Vanilla Party Cupcakes (page 59) and could even be used to sandwich two macaron halves together.

Makes 4 cups

2 cups (450 g) unsalted butter, room temperature

4 cups (500 g) confectioners' sugar

½ cup vanilla or white cake mix

3 tablespoons heavy (35%) cream, cold

2 teaspoons pure vanilla extract (or 1 teaspoon vanilla bean paste)

1. In the bowl of a stand mixer fitted with the paddle attachment, beat the butter on medium speed until creamy, about 30 seconds.

2. With the mixer running on low speed, gradually add the confectioners' sugar, 1 cup at a time, until incorporated. Add the cake mix and the cream. Turn the mixer up to medium speed and beat for about 2 minutes, until the frosting is light and fluffy. Stop the mixer and scrape down the sides and bottom of the bowl with a rubber spatula.

3. Add the vanilla, then beat on medium speed for 2 additional minutes.

4. Use immediately to frost cakes or cupcakes.

Royal Icing

I first learned about Royal Icing when I bought one of Peggy Porschen's cookbooks at my local bookstore. Before then, I had been using rolled fondant to decorate my cookies, but since I've never been a fondant fan, I was eager to explore an alternative. These days, Royal Icing is the only kind of icing I use to decorate my cookies. To learn how to decorate using Royal Icing, see page 110.

Makes 2 cups

White vinegar, for wiping mixer bowl and utensils

3¾ cups (465 g) confectioners' sugar

3 tablespoons meringue powder

¼ cup plus 1 teaspoon warm water, plus more to thin

1. Wipe the inside of a mixer bowl, as well as the paddle attachment, with white vinegar. (The acid in the vinegar will remove any greasy residue that might interfere with the drying of the icing.)

2. Place the sugar and meringue powder in the mixer bowl and mix together on low speed until combined. With the mixer running on low speed, add the water until the mixture is moist and mixes easily. If the mixture is a bit too thick, add a little more water.

3. Mix on low speed for 10 minutes. After this time, the icing will be very thick, will have doubled in volume and should hold a stiff peak. This is called "stiff peak" icing. It is usually used as an edible "glue" (think gingerbread houses) or for piping decorations.

4. To make "soft peak" icing, with the mixer running on low speed, add more water, a little at a time, until the icing holds soft peaks similar to the consistency of toothpaste. Soft-peak icing is ideal for piping borders, outlines and other details on cookies and cakes.

5. To make "flood" icing, with the mixer running on low speed, add more water, a little at a time, until the icing is runny. When drizzled back on itself, the ribbon of icing should disappear in 10 to 12 seconds, no more, no less. Flood-consistency icing is used to "flood," or fill in, cookies after outlining the edges with soft-peak icing.

6. While using your icing, keep any icing that you aren't using covered with a damp tea towel, as it dries out quickly.

7. Leftover icing will keep in the refrigerator, covered with a damp tea towel, for up to 24 hours. Bring it back to life by mixing on low speed with the paddle attachment.

Sweet Tip

1. Be careful not to thin out your flood icing too much. Otherwise, it will run right off of your cookies and create a sweet mess!

2. Keep icing that is drying away from water. A single drop of water on drying or dried icing will create a crater that can't be fixed.

3. Mind the humidity. If a room where royal icing is drying is too humid, the icing will have a tough time drying completely. I find that any room below 55 percent humidity is a safe zone. (If you're really serious about it, you can always purchase a dehumidifier to help suck up any excess moisture in the air.)

4. Speaking of humidity, don't crisscross-stack your baking sheets of iced decorations or cookies while they're drying. Inadequate airflow around the baking sheets, plus moisture buildup, equals improperly dried icing.

Chocolate Ganache

This easy recipe can be used in so many different ways! Use it to cover the Cookie Dough Chocolate Sprinkle Cake (page 34), whip it into Bake Shop Vanilla Frosting (page 190) or dip Sprinkly Chocolate Cake Doughnuts (page 148) into it.

Makes 2 cups

1½ cups (265 g) semi-sweet chocolate chips

1 cup heavy (35%) cream

1. Place the chocolate chips in a heatproof bowl.

2. Heat the cream in a saucepan over medium heat until it begins to bubble and is very hot. Carefully pour the hot cream over the chocolate chips. Allow the two to sit together for about 15 seconds, then whisk until smooth and well blended.

3. Use immediately or allow it to cool for about 20 minutes before scraping into an airtight container. Ganache will keep in the refrigerator for up to 3 days.

Sweet Sugar Glaze

This simple and versatile icing can be whipped up in a pinch. Use it to ice the Cherry Almond Fairy Cakes (page 86) or drizzle it over Lemon Delight Cookies (page 107). It can also be used as a drippy cake topping.

Makes 1 cup

2¼ cups (280 g) confectioners' sugar

¼ cup whole milk, room temperature

1. Place the sugar and milk in a medium bowl. Whisk together vigorously until smooth. Use immediately.

Variation
Lemon Glaze: Add 2 teaspoons lemon extract along with the milk.

Eggless Chocolate Chip Cookie Dough

I'm definitely guilty of eating raw cookie dough by the spoonful, but this eggless version is a much safer (and really delightful) option. Use it in the Cookie Dough Chocolate Sprinkle Cake (page 34) or as a filling between two cookies, like in my Cookie Dough Sandwich Cookies (page 101).

Makes 4 cups

2½ cups (315 g) all-purpose flour

Pinch of salt

1 cup (225 g) unsalted butter, room temperature

1 cup (220 g) packed brown sugar

¾ cup (150 g) granulated sugar

6 tablespoons whole milk, room temperature

2 teaspoons pure vanilla extract

1½ cups (265 g) semi-sweet chocolate chips

1. In a medium bowl, whisk together the flour and the salt. Set aside.

2. In the bowl of a stand mixer fitted with the paddle attachment, beat the butter and brown and granulated sugars on medium speed until light and fluffy, about 2 minutes. Stop the mixer and scrape down the sides and bottom of the bowl with a rubber spatula. Add the milk and vanilla, then beat again on medium speed to combine.

3. With the mixer running on low speed, add the flour mixture all at once. Once the flour is completely incorporated, stop the mixer and scrape down the sides and bottom of the bowl with a rubber spatula. Fold in the chocolate chips.

4. Cookie dough will keep in an airtight container in the refrigerator for up to 5 days.

Variation
Sprinkled Cookie Dough: Fold in ½ cup sprinkles with the chocolate chips.

Eggless Peanut Butter Cookie Dough

This decadent dough is the filling inside of the Cookie Dough Truffles (page 159) but would be wonderful in a cake, too. Try spreading it inside Chocolate Sprinkle Cake (page 31) or sandwiching it between Double Chocolate Cookies (page 98).

Makes 2 cups

1¾ cups (220 g) all-purpose flour

Pinch of salt

½ cup (115 g) unsalted butter, room temperature

½ cup (110 g) packed brown sugar

¼ cup (50 g) granulated sugar

3 tablespoons whole milk, room temperature

1 teaspoon pure vanilla extract

½ cup (120 g) smooth peanut butter

1. In a medium bowl, whisk together the flour and the salt. Set aside.

2. In the bowl of a stand mixer fitted with the paddle attachment, beat the butter and brown and granulated sugars on medium speed until light and fluffy, about 2 minutes. Stop the mixer and scrape down the sides and bottom of the bowl with a rubber spatula. Add the milk and vanilla, then beat again on medium speed to combine. Add the peanut butter and beat until smooth.

3. With the mixer running on low speed, add the flour mixture all at once. Once the flour is completely incorporated, stop the mixer and scrape down the sides and bottom of the bowl with a rubber spatula. Mix on low speed until combined.

4. Cookie dough will keep in an airtight container in the refrigerator for up to 5 days.

Vanilla Bean Whipped Cream

This heavenly topping can be whipped up in a pinch. Use it to top the Mint Chip Cheesecake Cups (page 143) or the Frozen Banana Split Cheesecake Cones (page 155) or anywhere else you'd use whipped cream.

Makes 1 cup

1 cup heavy (35%) cream, cold

½ teaspoon vanilla bean paste

½ teaspoon granulated sugar

1. In the bowl of a stand mixer fitted with the whisk attachment (or in a large bowl and using an electric beater), whip the cream with the vanilla bean paste on medium speed for about 1 minute. Sprinkle the sugar over the cream while whipping, then turn the mixer up to medium-high speed and whip until soft peaks form.

2. Use immediately or store in an airtight container in the refrigerator for up to 3 hours.

Blackberry Compote

This tasty compote can be used in so many different ways. Spoon it over Vanilla Blackberry Crumble Cupcakes (page 72), fold into Bake Shop Vanilla Frosting (page 190), drizzle it over ice cream or smooth it between cake layers.

Makes 1 cup

2 cups blackberries, fresh or frozen

½ cup (100 g) granulated sugar

1 cup water

1 teaspoon pure vanilla extract

Zest of ½ lemon

Pinch of salt

1. In a medium saucepan, stir together the blackberries, sugar, water, vanilla, lemon zest and salt. Place over medium-low heat and simmer for about an hour, or until the berries are very soft and the mixture has thickened slightly.

2. Remove from the heat and use the back of a fork or a potato masher to squish and mash up the berries. Allow the compote to cool completely.

3. Compote will keep in an airtight container in the refrigerator for up to 1 week.

Wonderful Caramel

Very few things make my kitchen smell more delightful than freshly made caramel, and once you've made your own, you'll be hooked. Caramel gets very, very hot while it cooks, so be sure to keep little hands away until it has completely cooled. Drizzle over Banana Caramel Supreme Cupcakes (page 77) or fold it into Bake Shop Vanilla Frosting (page 190) and pipe swirls onto the Carnival Caramel Popcorn Cupcakes (page 71).

Makes 1 cup

1 cup (200 g) granulated sugar

3 tablespoons water

6 tablespoons (85 g) unsalted butter, room temperature

½ cup heavy (35%) cream, room temperature

1 teaspoon pure vanilla extract

¼ teaspoon salt

1. Place the sugar and water in a medium saucepan. Over medium heat, stir constantly with a wooden spoon until the sugar has dissolved, then leave the mixture alone to bubble until it thickens and becomes amber in colour, about 10 minutes.

2. Add the butter and stir together until combined. Add the cream and stir constantly. The mixture will bubble up as soon as the cream is added. Stir until the caramel is smooth.

3. Remove the pan from the heat and stir in the vanilla and salt. Place a fine-mesh sieve over a heatproof bowl and strain the hot caramel to rid it of any lumps. Allow the caramel to cool completely. As it cools, it will thicken.

4. Caramel will keep in an airtight container in the refrigerator for up to 1 week.

Cookie Crumble

These buttery, sugary crumbs add a delightful little crunch to desserts. Toss them over cakes, sprinkle them onto fillings between cake layers or tuck them into the Vanilla Blackberry Crumble Cupcakes (page 72).

Makes 2 cups

1 cup (125 g) all-purpose flour

½ cup (100 g) granulated sugar

Pinch of salt

6 tablespoons (85 g) unsalted butter, melted

½ teaspoon pure vanilla extract

1. Preheat the oven to 350°F (180°C). Line a baking sheet with parchment paper.

2. In a medium bowl, whisk together the flour, sugar and salt. Add the melted butter and vanilla and mix together using a rubber spatula. The dough should be crumbly and hold together loosely. Dump the mixture onto the prepared baking sheet and spread it evenly.

3. Bake for 15 to 17 minutes, until the crumbs just begin to brown slightly. Allow the crumble to cool completely on the baking sheet.

4. Crumble will keep in an airtight container for up to 2 weeks.

Sources

Sprinkles, Glitter and Lustre Dust

Amazon (amazon.ca or amazon.com)

Bulk Barn (bulkbarn.ca)

CK Products (ckproducts.com)

Fancy Sprinkles (fancysprinkles.com)

Golda's Kitchen (goldaskitchen.com)

Gourmet Warehouse (gourmetwarehouse.ca)

Scoop-N-Save (scoop-n-save.com)

Tiny Kitchen Treats (tinykitchentreats.com)

Edible Markers and Paintbrushes

Michaels (michaels.com)

Scoop-N-Save (scoop-n-save.com)

Wilton (wilton.com)

Cookie Cutters

Cheap Cookie Cutters (cheapcookiecutters.com)

Scoop-N-Save (scoop-n-save.com)

Gel Food Colouring

AmeriColor (amcricolorcorp.com)

Gourmet Warehouse (gourmetwarehouse.ca)

Scoop-N-Save (scoop-n-save.com)

Cake Boards

Bulk Barn (bulkbarn.ca)

Golda's Kitchen (goldaskitchen.com)

Gourmet Warehouse (gourmetwarehouse.ca)

Scoop-N-Save (scoop-n-save.com)

Gourmet Baking Ingredients

Golda's Kitchen (goldaskitchen.com)

Gourmet Warehouse (gourmetwarehouse.ca)

Vanilla Food Company (vanillafoodcompany.ca)

Whole Foods Market (wholefoodsmarket.com)

Piping Tips and Pastry Bags

Ateco (atecousa.com)

Gourmet Warehouse (gourmetwarehouse.ca)

Michaels (michaels.com)

Ming Wo Cookware (mingwo.com)

Scoop-N-Save (scoop-n-save.com)

Wilton (wilton.com)

Edible Gold Leaf and Flakes

Golda's Kitchen (goldaskitchen.com)

Gourmet Warehouse (gourmetwarehouse.ca)

Bakeware and Equipment

Gourmet Warehouse (gourmetwarehouse.ca)

Hudson's Bay (thebay.com)

Ming Wo Cookware (mingwo.com)

Williams-Sonoma (williams-sonoma.com)

Cotton Candy

Fluffë (fluffe.com)

Thank You

As I sit here typing these words, I still can't believe it—is this really happening? I wrote a book?! Along the way, I've laughed a lot, I've cried a lot, too, and I've realized just how grateful I am to be here, doing what I love. That said, this book wouldn't have happened without the help, support and love of many people.

First, to the entire team at Penguin Random House Canada—thank you for everything you've done to bring this book to life.

To my editor, Andrea—I had been dreaming of writing a book for years. Thank you for believing in my desserts, in my brand and in me.

To my literary agent, Sharon, thank you for helping me navigate this crazy world of publishing and for always answering my many questions.

To my high school food teacher Ms. Lucy, for allowing me to have some creative freedom in class (this is what kids like myself needed!) and for putting up with my constant chatter.

To my friends Chelan and Nicolette, for your loyalty, for having my back from the bakery's beginning and for not killing me, even though at times I know you wanted to. Also for recipe tasting and testing—thank you!

To my friend Erin of Sparkle Media, for helping plan and style the lifestyle photos in this book and for being a great friend. Also, a big thank you to your husband, Roberto, for helping with so many projects and for wearing pink pants without hesitation—a man who wears pink without complaining is a true gem!

To my friend and makeup artist Suzanna of Tori Blush, for always bending your schedule to fit mine and for making me feel truly beautiful, each and every time.

To my photographer and friend Kristy of Blush Wedding Photography, for helping bring my sweet dreams to life. Your photography talents are out of this world and you are truly a pleasure to work with. Thank you for going above and beyond what was asked—you are amazing!

To my friend Pam, thank you for letting me take over your beautiful home while shooting photos for this book. I know that it wasn't easy and I truly appreciate it, so much.

To Daveney, thank you for being such a great little helper in the kitchen. Also, a big sugary thank you to your mom, dad and brother for rearranging their schedules to have you be a part of that sweet day.

To my friend Sarah, for cooking me dinners and for taste-testing countless desserts. Also for letting me come over to drink wine in my sweats and vent and for always being honest with me.

To Austin, my sweet, sweet dog. I'm well aware that you can't read, but I still want to acknowledge your part in this book. Thank you for cleaning crumbs off the floor and for putting up with my endless requests for you to wear party hats.

To my parents, Carol and Phil, for always telling me that I can do anything I set my mind to. I can't explain how much it means to me to have grown up with such a strong support system. Also, thanks for washing dishes in my bakery all day on your wedding anniversary and for babysitting my sweet Austin so that I could pursue my dreams.

To Dorian, for always believing in my wild ideas and helping bring them to life. Your generosity will never, ever be forgotten. I'll love you for always.

And last but not least, to all of the Sweet Bake Shop customers, thank you from the bottom of my heart for supporting my business. Without you, I wouldn't have written this book.

Macaron Templates

Cotton Candy Cloud Macaron Template (page 206, below)

Basic French Macaron Template (page 207, opposite page)

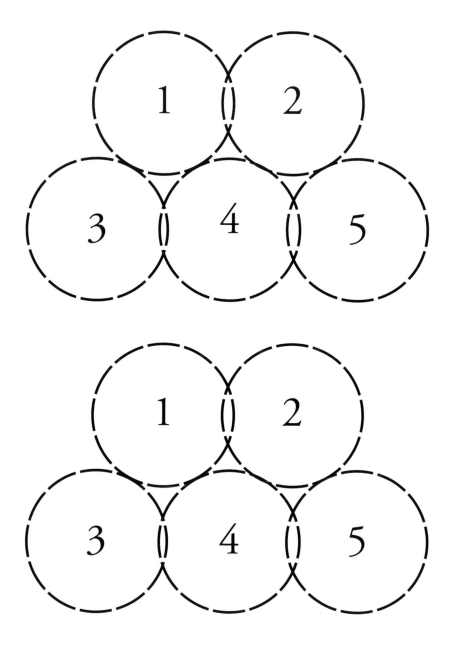

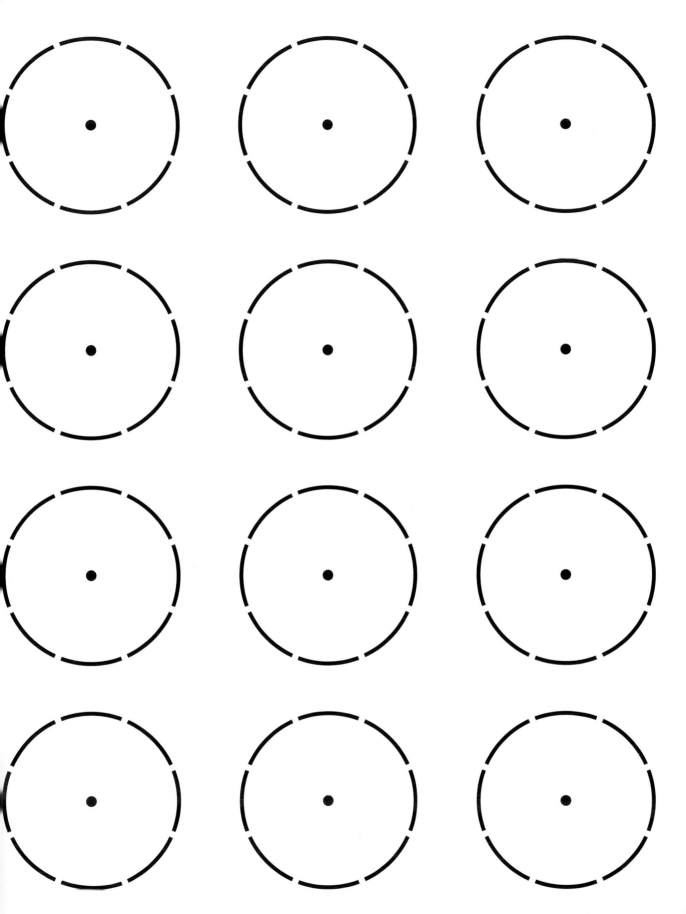

Index

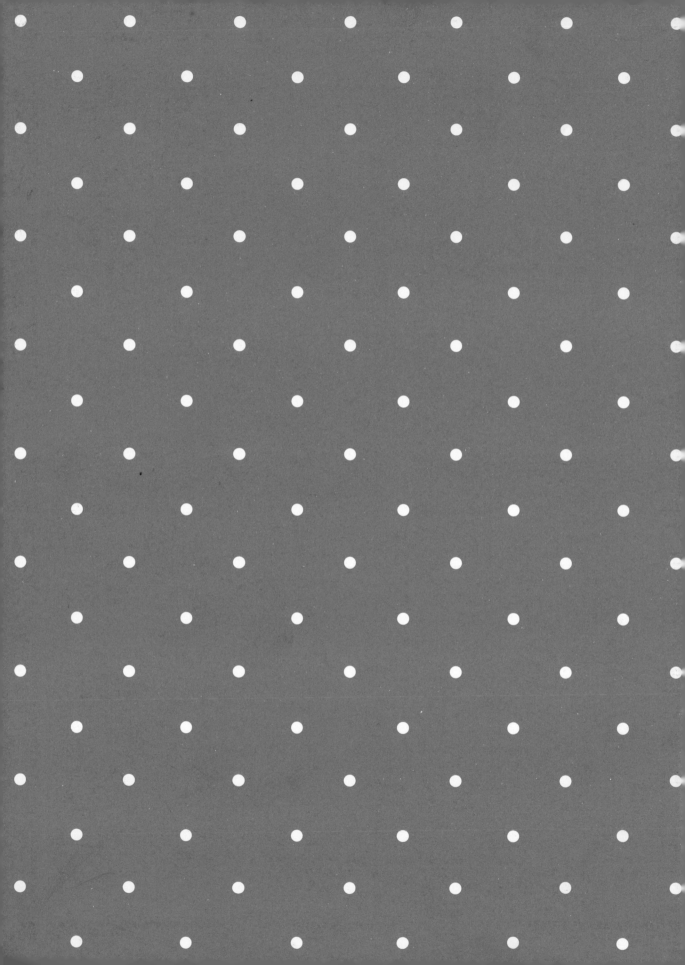

Luke Goes to Bat

RACHEL ISADORA

G. P. Putnam's Sons
New York

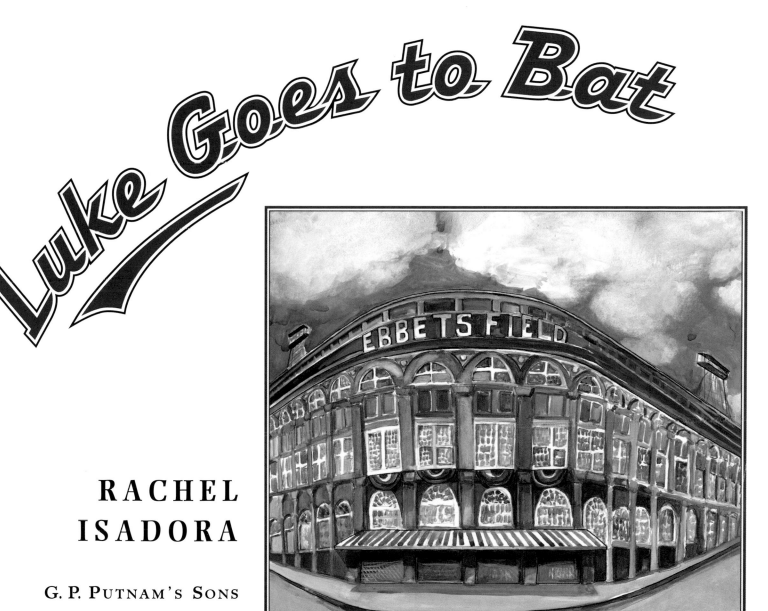

For Nicholas "39"

The game in this story is based on an actual one that took place
in Philadelphia between the Dodgers and the Phillies in 1951.
In the fourteenth inning, after a ball and a strike, Jackie Robinson
hit a home run that won the game, 9–8, for the Dodgers.

Published simultaneously in Canada.
Manufactured in China by South China Printing Co. Ltd.
Designed by Cecilia Yung and Gunta Alexander. Text set in Administer.
The art was done in (tk).
Library of Congress Cataloging-in-Publication Data
Isadora, Rachel. Luke goes to bat / Rachel Isadora. p. cm.
Summary: Luke is not very good at baseball, but his grandmother and
sports star Jackie Robinson encourage him to keep trying.
[1. Baseball—Fiction. 2. Perseverance (Ethics)—Fiction. 3. Robinson,
Jackie, 1919–1972—Fiction. 4. Grandmothers—Fiction.] I. Title.
PZ7.I763Luk 2005 [E]—dc22 2004001890 ISBN 0-399-23604-X
10 9 8 7 6 5 4 3 2 1 First Impression

It was Brooklyn.

It was summer.

It was baseball.

All day long the kids on Bedford Avenue
played stickball in the streets.

Except for Luke.

"When you're older," his big brother, Nicky, told him.

"He's just a squirt," one of the other kids said, laughing.

So Luke watched the games from the curb, and then he'd practice.

He threw a ball against the wall next to the deli. He practiced his swing over and over again. He ran as fast as he could up and down the block.

He wanted to be ready when it was time.

And at night, whenever the
Dodgers were playing, Luke hurried
up to the roof, where he could see
the lights of Ebbets Field. When
he heard the crowd go wild, he
imagined his favorite player, Jackie
Robinson, had hit a home run.

Someday, Luke thought, I will
hit a home run, too.

Finally, one morning, the team was short a player.

"Franky had to go to his aunt's!"

"Who we gonna get?"

"Hey," said Luke, "what about me?"

Everyone was quiet.

"Aw, come on," said his brother. "Give him a chance."

"We got nobody else."

"He better not mess up."

They put him in left field. No balls came his way, so he just stood there.

When it was his turn up at bat, Luke took a few practice swings, then stepped up to the plate.

"I'll show them," Luke muttered.

The ball whizzed past.

"Strike one!"

Luke held the bat higher.

"Strike two!"

Luke was barely in position when the next ball flew past and the catcher yelled, "Out!"

"You stink," Luke heard.

He got up to bat one more time but struck out again.

"Sometimes it just goes that way," his brother told him.

Franky came back in the afternoon, so Luke spent the rest of the day on the curb. He was sure they'd never let him play again.

Grandma was in the kitchen when he got home.

"I finally got a chance to play with the team," Luke told her.

Grandma could tell that the game hadn't gone well. "Not everyone plays like Jackie Robinson all the time," she said. "Not even Jackie Robinson."

Luke didn't smile.

"By the way," Grandma said, "are you doing anything tomorrow night?"

Luke shrugged.

"Well, if you're so busy, someone else will have to go with me to the game at Ebbets Field."

"What? You mean a real game?"

Grandma held up two tickets.

Ebbets Field was ablaze with lights. But this time, Luke didn't have to imagine the game.

"Thanks for taking me, Grandma," he said.

They watched the Dodgers and Phillies battle it out. The game went into extra innings. By the time the Dodgers got up to bat in the bottom of the fourteenth inning, the score was still tied, 8–8. With two outs, Jackie Robinson was up.

The crowd roared.

"Come on, Jackie!" Luke yelled.

The pitcher threw a curveball. Jackie swung.

"Strike one!" the umpire called.

The pitcher wound up. He threw a fastball and Jackie missed.

"Strike two!"

Three balls followed.

All eyes at Ebbets Field rested on Jackie. The Dodgers could still win.

Luke shouted with the crowd. "Give it to 'em, Jackie! You show 'em!"

Jackie looked around from under his cap, then dug his feet into the dirt.

The pitcher began his windup.

"You can do it, Jackie," Luke whispered. "You can do it."

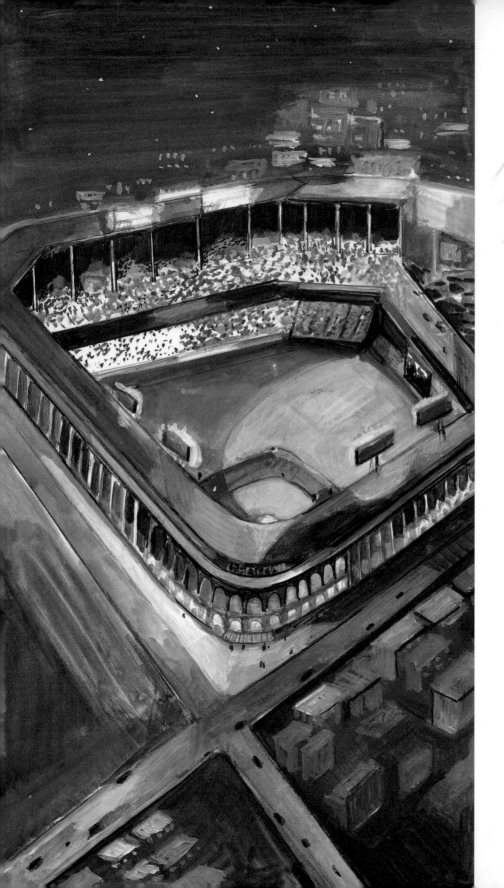

Suddenly, Luke heard the loud crack of a bat. When he looked up, the ball was flying over his head, flying over the scoreboard, flying over the walls of Ebbets Field! The crowd went wild!

Luke stood up on his seat and cheered, "You showed 'em, Jackie!"

"What a game!" Grandma said. "See, you can't give up. Even Jackie Robinson's got to keep trying."

Luke didn't answer.

When Luke got home, he ran up to the roof. The lights were going out at Ebbets Field.

"Come on down! It's bedtime!" Nicky called.

Just then, Luke saw a ball lying on the ground.

"Look!" he said, picking it up. "This is the home run ball that Jackie Robinson hit tonight!"

"Naw. That's just some old ball a kid hit up on the roof," Nick said, laughing, as he went downstairs.

And that's when Luke saw him.
It was Jackie Robinson himself.
"I hit that one for you, kid."
Before Luke could say a word,
Jackie ran to the dugout to join
the other Dodgers. But he looked
back one more time.

"Hey, kid," he said. "Your grandma was right. You can't give up."

"Thanks, Mr. Robinson."

The final lights went out at Ebbets Field. Luke looked down at the winning ball and smiled.

"I won't," he whispered to himself.

And he didn't.

10 May 05